POWER AND AUTHORITY

Transformation of Campus Governance

Harold L. Hodgkinson

L. Richard Meeth

EDITORS

POWER AND AUTHORITY

Jossey-Bass Inc., Publishers
615 Montgomery Street · San Francisco · 1971

POWER AND AUTHORITY
Transformation of Campus Governance
Harold L. Hodgkinson and L. Richard Meeth, Editors

Jossey-Bass, Inc., Publishers
615 Montgomery Street
San Francisco, California 94111

Library of Congress Catalog Card Number 74-132821

International Standard Book Number ISBN 0-87589-079-2

Manufactured in the United States of America
Composed and printed by York Composition Company, Inc.
Bound by Chas. H. Bohn & Co., Inc.

JACKET DESIGN BY WILLI BAUM, SAN FRANCISCO

FIRST EDITION

Code 7027

The Jossey-Bass Series in Higher Education

General Editors

JOSEPH AXELROD
San Francisco State College and University of California, Berkeley

MERVIN B. FREEDMAN
San Francisco State College and Wright Institute, Berkeley

Preface

If, as Robert Frost says, freedom is "working easy in harness," then power is the horse and authority the hand on the plow. The plow, the instrument of fulfillment, needs both power and authority to accomplish its task. We understand power as the force and authority as the mandate or right that moves institutions of higher learning. Carrying the analogy one step further, we also differentiate between government and governance, government being the plow, the instrument, or the entity to be moved, and governance being the act of plowing or the process of governing by setting freedom, power, and authority loose in the production of furrows.

Major new forces have been unloosed on our society; we

are indeed in transition—but from what? To what? Now, as in all times of rapid social change, we disagree on the answers. Yet there is clearly a change in our reflexive loyalty to social institutions, our conceptions of legitimate power and authority, and our assumptions as to what participation in government means, both for the organization and for the individual.

It is a difficult time for the leadership of any organization: Student protests parallel wildcat labor strikes, which take place after union leadership has settled with management. Many young clergymen cannot follow the dictates of the church hierarchy. Every organization seems to be facing a crisis of confidence. Leaders can no longer count upon being obeyed reflexively.

Student protests have exposed for public view some of the most private and personal aspects of the ways in which institutions of higher education are governed. The same thing may happen in the world of business as students acquire stock shares and vote proxies in new ways. But at the moment the structure of colleges and universities has been bared for public view. The structure can be looked at in at least two different dimensions: By looking at the organization charts, we can get a static view of the positions which constitute the structure. This can be called the government of the institution. Or, we can look at the people who occupy the positions on the charts and watch how they operate. This process of individuals working through positions can be called governance.

The range of views expressed by our authors is as broad as the range of opinion now current within the education profession. And each day, as new events take place which have direct implications for campus governance, people shift their views. There are no rights and wrongs in the field at the present time. But public institutions of higher education may end up being governed from the outside by political forces if faculty, students, and administrators prove unable to govern them from inside.

Our authors view higher education as a political system. At least since Socrates people have judged the relative merits of political systems in terms of the relationship of power and authority and until the twentieth century saw little reason to define concepts which were judged to be common knowledge. In this century, however, sociologists, notably Max Weber, have felt the need to distinguish elements, characteristics, types, and effects of power (generally conceived to be the superordinate concept).

This volume is a compilation of papers from two sources: a conference on power in college government sponsored by Higher Education Executive Associates (HEEA) and a set of papers commissioned by the Carnegie Foundation for the Advancement of Teaching, dealing with campus governance. We are especially grateful to Thomas Emmet of HEEA for permission to print these papers and to Margot Hartman for endless thankless hours of typing. We hope that these statements will encourage "working easy in harness."

Berkeley, California HAROLD L. HODGKINSON
Kansas City, Missouri L. RICHARD MEETH
September 1970

Contents

Authors

DANIEL BELL, professor of sociology, Harvard University

KINGMAN BREWSTER, JR., president, Yale University

RODNEY T. HARTNETT, research psychologist, Educational Testing Service

HAROLD L. HODGKINSON, research educator and project director, Center for Research and Development in Higher Education, Berkeley

RAY A. HOWE, dean of faculty, Henry Ford Community College, and director of labor relations, Dearborn, Michigan, Community College District

RALPH K. HUITT, executive director, National Association of State Universities and Land-Grant Colleges

ROBERT JOHNSTON, graduate student, School of Public and International Affairs, Princeton University

T. R. McCONNELL, professor of higher education, University of California, Berkeley

EARL J. McGRATH, director, Higher Education Center, Temple University

L. RICHARD MEETH, consultant to small colleges

ROBERT S. POWELL, JR., graduate student, Princeton University

WALTER SCHENKEL, research associate, Center for Research and Development in Higher Education, Berkeley

POWER AND AUTHORITY

Transformation of Campus Governance

It is an observation no less just than common that there is no stronger test of a man's real character than power and authority, exciting as they do every passion and discovering every latent vice.

Plutarch

1

Walter Schenkel

Who Has Been in Power?

The emergence of the American university has been the subject of numerous studies, although no study has specifically focused on university governance as it grew to become the highly complex organization it is today. This short chapter does not claim to provide such a history; rather, it will attempt only to select a few significant changes that have taken place in the governance configuration.

The American university emerged in the decades following the Civil War, when it became an institution that differed from the college of the pre-Civil War period. The early university had none of the complexity of its contemporary counterpart, but it was nevertheless different from its predecessor. The university not only enrolled more students than did the college, but also offered a wider range of subjects taught by a larger faculty. At first it did not have such characteristics of the modern university as graduate programs, professional schools, departmental structure, and research, all of which emerged later in the nineteenth century as distinctive features of the university. The main difference between the pre-Civil War college and the post-Civil War university, from the viewpoint of governance, was the change from an institutional control that was primarily sectarian to a control that was primarily secular—whether private or public. This change in control was very likely the major reason for the substantial widening of the early university constituencies, which had been rather narrow for the old college because of its sectarian and local base.

This chapter discusses those institutional changes in universities that are specifically related to changes in the governance configuration. *Governance* is here defined as the process of direct control by groups or individuals over university policies. Groups or individuals which attempt to control the university indirectly (such as legislatures and different interest groups) through one or several of the direct participants are not discussed. Among the groups or individuals that have through time exercised direct control over universities, some have been continuously part of the governance configuration, such as the governing board and the president, while others, such as students and faculty, emerged only lately as participants in the process of university governance. A third catgeory includes organizations such as government agencies and accrediting bodies, which influence university governance only periodically through review procedures. The role of the donors and especially the founders in the history of the American university was very important in the early days, although the founder has since passed from the center stage as a participant. All four types are discussed since they all participated or still participate directly in the process of university governance.

In 1902, in his decennial report to the trustees of the University of Chicago, President William R. Harper stated on the subject of a donor's participation in university governance: "A donor has the privilege of ceasing to make his gifts to an institution if, in his opinion, for any reason the work of the institution is not satisfactory; but as a *donor* he has no right to interfere with the administration of the university."[1] Most presidents of private universities founded in the second half of the nineteenth century would have wholeheartedly agreed with Harper's statement and most certainly would have extended it to include the founder of the university as well. Of all actors in the governance configuration of the early American university, none was potentially more influential than that small group of individuals who both founded and endowed a university. Some of the most prestigious private universities established in the nineteenth century were founded and endowed by a single individual. Such large-scale philanthropy became possible only when men who had accumulated fortunes decided to invest part of them in charitable projects in the form of universities or foundations, primarily as monuments to themselves and to their success. A number of these new universities received endowments which were remarkable even by present standards of the multimillion-dollar university.

An act of philanthropy such as the founding and endowing of a university obviously gave the donor a high degree of control, or at least potential control, over that university. A founder had different options with respect to the role he wanted to play in the governance configuration of his university. The possible options ranged from complete abstention to a continuous participation in all aspects of the governance process. Of the private universities founded in the second half of the nineteenth century, the cases of Cornell University (founded in 1868) and Stanford University (founded in 1891) are the most illustrative because they represent two diametrically opposed modes of behavior.

Andrew D. White, not Ezra Cornell, had the idea of founding the institution which was to become Cornell University. White and Cornell knew each other from the New York State legislature, of which both were members. White was a dynamic academic who had developed the idea of founding a university which would incorporate the best features of the different European universities. Cornell, on the other hand, had never gone to college. He started his career as a mechanic and became a very wealthy businessman who let it be known that he wanted to donate a substantial sum of money for a worthwhile cause. White approached Cornell when he heard of his intention and eventually persuaded him to donate his money for the establishment of a new university in Ithaca. Because of their different backgrounds, both men had different ideas of what purpose the university should serve. Cornell was primarily interested in a university which would be open to everybody regardless of social background and which would offer the widest possible range of subjects. White's plan was to found an institution which would strive for academic excellence. Their ideas were compatible, however, because White also intended to add technical curricula to the humanities. Since White not only had been the first to develop the Cornell idea but also seemed capable of turning the idea into reality, Cornell was content to entrust the whole task of establishing the new university to him. Cornell devoted himself to raising additional funds for the university and did not attempt to participate in governance. Cornell trusted White so completely that he let the president of the new university choose half the members of the board of trustees, a unique episode in the history of American higher education.

Unlike Cornell, Leland Stanford, the California railroad tycoon, did not have to be convinced that he should found and endow a university. Stanford decided that a university would be the most appropriate monument to his son, who had died in Europe. Once he had conceived the idea of a "living mausoleum," Stanford searched for a man to head the proposed university. He selected David Starr Jordan, who had been president of Indiana University. The educational ideals of Stanford and his equally strong-willed wife, Jane Lathrop Stanford, differed somewhat, but both were basically in favor of a vocationally oriented institution that would also attempt to build character. Jordan had a strong personality himself but conformed to the Stanfords' will and built the university according to their wishes. For a number of years the ultimate authority over the institution was vested not in a governing board but rather in the Stanfords. After Stanford's death, his wife remained the sole ruler and guided the destiny of the university with a determined but not very experienced hand, continuously intervening in the exercise of Jordan's prerogatives. Jordan was totally dedicated to the university but had frequent clashes with Jane Stanford, especially in matters of academic freedom, a concept which was totally alien to her. The most famous academic freedom instance was that of Professor Edward A. Ross, who aroused Jane Stanford's ire by working for the Democrats and propagating socialist ideals. After a long series of disputes, she finally succeeded in forcing Jordan to fire Ross. The Ross case was only one among many incidents in which Jane Stanford openly decided to hire or to fire faculty. She also was solely responsible for a very ambitious building program which left little money for current expenditures such as faculty salaries; at times the faculty seemed to be on the brink of famine. In short, there was no single area of governance in which Jane Stanford did not make the major decisions herself. Because of heavy criticism from all sides and the apparent state of disarray in which her heavy-handed rule left the university, Mrs. Stanford finally decided in 1903 to relinquish her absolute control over the university to a board of trustees.

These two examples demonstrate the ways in which a founder could either actively participate in the governance of his university or abstain from doing so. Cornell's decision to abstain but to give an enormous amount of power to a strong and farsighted president sharing basically the founder's educational ideals turned out to be beneficial for the university. The Stanfords' decision to assume many of the tasks of both trustees and president—tasks in which they had no experience—proved to be a serious error.

The case of donors was somewhat different from that of the founder because a donor had potentially fewer occasions to participate in university governance. However, Harper's complaint about donors who tried to influence university policies reveals that donors did in fact think that their gift gave them a certain amount of say in university governance. This belief was especially marked in the case of large donors who were also trustees. However, the tendency for donors to insist on participating in university governance is now considerably less marked than it was in the early university.[2] Modern universities have been successful in convincing donors to accept prestige instead of a share in governance, as the increasing number of endowed chairs indicates.

As with founders and donors, the trustees were an important element in American higher education from the establishment of the first colonial college. The basic function of the trustees and their corporate body, the governing board, was and still is to act as the guardian of the charter of an institution and to constitute the body in which ultimate authority is vested. Apart from this functional characteristic of the governing board, an organizational characteristic has remained the same: a governing board is not physically located on campus, and its members are usually not part of the student body, the faculty, or the administration.

Most of the predecessors of the university in this country were special-interest colleges which had been established to serve a well-defined constituency, such as a religious denomination. These institutions usually served a certain geographic area as well and had been founded for the primary purpose of providing higher education for the sons and daughters of, say, Methodists in Ohio. The trustees of such institutions were members of the group which had established the college, and because of sectarian sponsorship a large proportion of trustees were ministers. There is no evidence that specific knowledge, such as business experience, was then regarded as an essential qualification of trustees. For the denominational college, it was more important to have men who were loyal church members and who felt committed to the institution. In most pre-Civil War colleges the subjects taught, primarily theology and the humanities, did not require extensive facilities or a large number of professors. These colleges were thus relatively simple institutions that operated on small budgets and could easily be administered by boards of trustees which had no special business experience.

The universities established after the Civil War were somewhat more complex institutions than the previous ones. They enrolled more students, taught more subjects, employed more professors, and in addition offered graduate programs, which were not characteristic of the early institutions. (Clark University and Johns Hopkins University were exceptions, both having been established as graduate institutions.) The composition of the governing boards of the early universities did not differ much from that of colleges, but this situation was not to remain for long. As universities expanded in size and complexity, their budgets began to be measured in hundreds of thousands rather than in thousands of dollars. This change, and the fact that most universities were under secular control, accounts for the gradual disappearance of clergymen from governing boards and their replacement by individuals such as businessmen or lawyers, who could offer some useful skills. By the end of the nineteenth century, the governing boards of universities resembled the governing boards of business enterprises and had evolved many of their present characteristics. Their members tended to be college graduates, middle-aged or older and therefore experienced, successful in their professional life, and conservative in their attitudes. The membership of governing boards was professional because its members were recruited from the ranks of lawyers and businessmen, whose training made them an asset for the university. These trustees were also valued for a different reason—because board membership was regarded as prestigious, the trustees were expected not only to donate their time and their special skills but also to provide money or to have access to potential donors.[3] This was particularly true for private universities. It is likely that the early trustees of state universities were expected to maintain good relationships with legislators.

The areas of governance in which the trustees of many universities were most influential emerged gradually during the nineteenth century. The trustees' single most important prerogative was the election of the president, and the other major areas of their governance were personnel matters (appointment of faculty and senior administrators, questions of tenure, and so forth), educational policy, finance, and physical plant. As many boards were large, a division of labor permitted individual trustees to devote themselves to the questions in which they were most interested. This division of labor was institutionalized at a rather early stage since it became quite common for boards to distribute the work among standing committees. A good example is the board of trustees of the University of Chicago, which established at the outset a committee which dealt with all areas of instruction, a committee which managed the buildings and grounds, and a committee which supervised expenditures.[4] Although the early participants in the governance process quickly realized that most decisions in the area of educational programs should be left to the faculty, decisions regarding fundamental educational policies were invariably taken by the governing board.

The division of labor within the board of trustees of the University of Chicago was quite advanced. In most universities the tasks were less clearly defined and at times more narrowly construed. Trustees sometimes examined course reading lists, checking for books of which they did not approve. Whether other governing boards exercised more or less influence than the board at the University of Chicago depended not so much on the initiative of the trustees as on the relative influence of either the president or the founder of a university. At Clark and Stanford, the boards had very little influence in any area of governance as long as Jonas Clark or Jane Stanford assumed the tasks of both the president and the governing board. And at universities such as Ohio and West Virginia, which were headed by comparatively weak presidents, trustees were able to act like petty tyrants.[5]

Governing boards were traditionally conservative in attitudes and revealed this conservatism in many ways. It often made for a strong antagonism between president and board. Sometimes the trustees realized too late that the man chosen to be the chief executive of their university had political views or adhered to economic doctrines which were incompatible with their own, as in the case of E. Benjamin Andrews, who was fired from the presidency of Brown University because he advocated the free coinage of silver. In order to keep close control over the president, some governing boards appointed their chief executive by means of contracts that were renewable at short intervals. Their conservative values also were reflected in the way they dealt with academic freedom cases. President Arthur T. Hadley of Yale University argued that the moral consensus of the trustees was against giving license to professors.[6]

A basic ambivalence in the role of the trustee has not been resolved to this day. Is the trustee responsible to the university or to groups outside the university? The question is generally less acute for private universities with self-perpetuating boards of trustees, which tend to see themselves as carrying the ultimate responsibility for their institution. For example, in Catholic higher education the universities and colleges are often the creation of religious orders, and trustees frequently serve as watchdogs over the institution rather than as representatives of the university to the outside. In contrast, members of governing boards of public universities face dilemmas which their colleagues at private universities hardly know. Does a trustee appointed by the state represent the interests of the public to the university, or does he basically defend the interests of the university against the public opinion of the moment? State governments vested the ultimate authority over state universities in an independent body, a fact that suggests that legislatures recognized the necessity of a measure of independence for state universities. This principle is still recognized in theory, although in practice it is sometimes undermined. This aberration is borne out in the changes that have occurred in the composition of the board of regents of the University of California. Traditionally, members of the governing board, even though public appointees, saw their role as that of spokesmen for the university. Their view was not challenged when the educational philosophies of the governor, the legislature, and the different constituent groups of the university did not clash. With an increasing discrepancy among educational philosophies, however, clashes were bound to appear since outgoing members of the governing board were replaced by individuals more likely to see their role as that of a watchdog over the university. As a body, the governing board of a public university can therefore be either a defender or a censor of the university, depending on the political climate in which individuals are appointed to board membership.

Governing boards of universities have traditionally been

composed of individuals who are not members of student body, faculty, or administration. Whereas the faculty has in some instances been represented on governing boards, this practice did not become widespread until the late 1960s. Student representation on governing boards has been an alien idea, but this situation is changing as the example of the City University of New York in appointing some students is followed by other institutions. Greater student and faculty representation on governing boards might eventually result in a greater degree of responsiveness by trustees to the needs of all the constituencies of their institution, although many questions of accountability and conflict of interest must be resolved.

Important as the trustees have been, no individual has had a greater impact on the development of the American university than the president. Presidents of American universities in the nineteenth century were often true entrepreneurs in the field of higher education, and, like entrepreneurs in the business world, they sometimes became virtual dictators ruling an empire which they themselves had built up. Thorstein Veblen's description of these men as "captains of learning" was very much to the point, although not all presidents were fortunate enough to rule their institution with unlimited power. In many cases the authority of the president was severely curtailed by strong trustees and by the founders of the institution.

It can be argued that the rapid development of the American university during the nineteenth century was largely due to the relative freedom of action which many presidents enjoyed. Compared with European university heads, who had to contend with great faculty strength and relatively limited freedom of action, presidents of American universities were usually given a considerable degree of power in shaping the development of their institutions. Although certainly a number of pre-Civil War colleges were headed by strong presidents, the relatively small size of those institutions did not provide much scope for ambitious men, whose turn came with the establishment of the universities. As in other competitive businesses, some men were successful and some failed. President Henry P. Tappan of the University of Michigan ruined his career and almost ruined the university because he did not tolerate any challenges to his authority. He was unable to delegate power and thus failed to build up a cabinet of top aides who could have relieved him of much routine work. According to White, who had taught at the University of Michigan during Tappan's presidency, Tappan treated the members of the governing board like "mere ciphers." Tappan also was unfortunate in his treatment of the faculty and the state legislature, and thus seems to have had few allies.

White, the first president of Cornell University, was one of the first truly successful university presidents. His far-sightedness together with the unequaled amount of power given to him by Cornell made it possible for him to become an innovator in higher education on a large scale. He emphasized that a university president needs to delegate authority, and as a result he created a cabinet of top aides and a division of labor which is still in use today. Since he was able to appoint half of the members of the board of trustees, he chose men with whom he could easily cooperate. He also sought the advice of the faculty in matters of appointments. Although White had a very strong personality, he was not usually described as a despot, a term which could accurately describe many other university presidents, particularly in the last decade of the nineteenth century. Harper of the University of Chicago started his career as president of that university in an auspicious manner by personally raiding the faculty of ailing Clark University, causing Clarke's president, G. Stanley Hall, to beg him to leave at least a skeleton faculty.[7]

White and Harper were undoubtedly the single most influential figures in the governance configurations of their respective universities, but they were not necessarily typical of the majority of university presidents in the nineteenth century. In some of the smaller universities, the board of trustees was more influential in university governance than was the president. But in no case was the president's authority as curtailed as in those universities in which the founder insisted on participating in all areas of governance, such as at Stanford University in the early years. At Stanford, the situation contained built-in conflict because Jordan was himself a strong and autocratic man who was unable to see the advantages of finding an ally among the faculty. Like Harper at Chicago, Jordan denied his faculty any voice in appointment matters. He disliked the idea of letting the faculty participate in any matter of consequence and was known to oppose the idea of tenure and the concept of autonomous departments. Furthermore, he disliked the idea of delegating authority to top aides such as deans.[8] This lack of allies put Jordan at a strong disadvantage in his relations with the Stanfords. The position of Hall at Clark was even more vulnerable. The financial situation of the university was precarious since Clark never gave the university the full endowment he had promised and since the income from student fees was very low because of a small enrollment. During the whole length of his disappointing tenure as president of Clark, Hall at least had the satisfaction of working with a board of trustees which, though rather weak, backed him.

Once the universities had become fully established, the scope for academic entrepreneurship diminished. The career of Nicholas Murray Butler, whose presidency at Columbia University began in the early years of the twentieth century and lasted for several decades, was more like that of the "captains of learning" of the late nineteenth century than of his contemporaries who headed other universities. During the period of consolidation which followed the expansion of the late nineteenth century, presidents of universities and industries were more likely to be executives managing an established organization rather than entrepreneurs building an empire. Governance in the contemporary American university is a complex system of checks and balances in which it is virtually impossible for a single person to dominate the governance process. The reason is found in the emergence of the professional managers.

Of all the roles in university governance, the administration, the professional managerial group, is now the most ubiquitous in terms of its range of functions and its degree of influence. Accounts of the early days of the university in the United States do not usually distinguish between administrative actions taken by the president and those taken by his top aides. The terms *president* and *administration* are usually treated as if they were synonymous. This treatment indicates that administrators constituted an appendix to presidential power instead of functioning as actors in their own right. Administrators in universities moved from backstage to center stage over a time span corresponding to the managerial revolution in business organizations. Two major periods can be identified. The first lasted approximately from the post-Civil War era to the early 1890s. During this formative period of the American university, administrative staffs were small and their functions were limited. The second period began in the early 1890s, when the administration as an entity took on new functions and increased in size, a result of the increasing enrollments and the diversification of the universities. Only at this point did the administration develop into a large-scale bureaucracy. Veblen's criticism of the university president as an entrepreneur in higher education refers to this period, when administrations often became empires with the president at the apex. A president with a specialized corps of administrators at hand could exercise power in many more areas than could his predecessor in the early university.

Where did these administrators originate? Before the emergence of the early university, in the days of the pre-Civil War college, the president was usually the principal faculty member, administrator, educator (who personally looked after the welfare and extracurricular activities of his students), fund raiser, record keeper, and accountant. The president of the larger, more complex university was of course unable to carry out all these functions, so he had to find people to whom he could delegate most of these tasks. It was natural that the president's choice for top administrative aides fell on faculty members. White of Cornell nominated from among the faculty three men who showed administrative abilities for the posts of vice-president, registrar, and secretary. Cornell may have been the first American university to adopt this division of labor, which has since become the accepted pattern. The positions of bursar and dean appeared soon after. The delegation of authority to top aides freed the president from routine tasks and made it possible for him to spend more time representing the university to the outside or even to take long leaves of absence from the university, as did White. Such a delegation of authority to top aides necessarily led to a consolidation of their position.

More indirect is the authority of the alumni. They have never been among the major participants in the governance configuration of the American university but have nevertheless traditionally been able to exert influence in some areas of governance, primarily through alumni groups and associations. Since the establishment of universities in this country, alumni have been a continuous source of financial and moral support to their alma maters. Private universities did, and still do, derive a substantial proportion of their income from alumni donations. State universities, too, have traditionally enlisted the support of their graduates in fund-raising activities, generally for projects that could not ordinarily be financed through state appropriations, such as alumni houses and other nonessential buildings, sports, and student affairs. The principal function of the alumni remains to attract money and talent from the outside world to their university. This support has come principally from those graduates feeling a sense of loyalty that was created primarily during their undergraduate years, a period when the total experience of college life is more important to the student than it is on the more task-oriented graduate level. Failure to stress undergraduate education usually had negative effects on the volume of alumni contributions. Thus, the failure of two universities—Clark University and Johns Hopkins University—to become financially viable as pure graduate schools would seem to be the result not only of insufficient endowments and student fees but of insufficient alumni support as well.

Other universities established in the nineteenth century did not share this problem because they started out as undergraduate institutions and evolved graduate programs later. Alumni influence in many of these institutions was considerable. The most interesting case of a direct causal relationship between alumni influence and increased revenue is that of the early University of Michigan. The president, Tappan, found it difficult to obtain sufficient annual appropriations from the state legislature for his university, probably because of the small number of college-educated men in the legislature. However, money started to flow much more freely when an increasing number of state legislators were elected from among the graduates.[9]

The alumni soon realized that in return for their direct support (through donations) or indirect support (through applying pressure on the state legislature) they could become part of the governance configuration. Many universities gave the alumni a certain amount of authority, either by permitting them to elect representatives to the governing board or by giving them virtual control over some matters. The second type of participation was more prevalent than the first, and even today in the majority of universities the alumni control many of the sports activities, including sponsoring fellowships for athletes and controlling the appointment of coaches. Such control over sports served the dual purpose of renewing the loyalty of alumni to their institution and of constituting the most important public relations effort among alumni.

But alumni influence has not been limited to the area of sports, though it was most visible in that area. Alumni have at times been able to exercise strong influence in the areas of educational programs and student affairs. Because of their knowledge of the university from the student perspective, they have often shown strong support for student demands. Alumni influence was innovative when student demands were innovative, and conservative when student demands were conservative. Thus, when Jordan tried to combat increasing student hedonism which resulted in the "liquor rebellion" at Stanford University, the alumni sided with the students. At Yale, the alumni forced the university to abandon the idea of honors programs because they—and the students—felt that the honors concept would discriminate against the average student. At Princeton University, alumni influence was innovative when the alumni forced the university in the 1890s to introduce the long-overdue elective principle.

When the American university emerged in the post-Civil War era, faculty participation in governance was unheard of. Faculty members in the early university were employees hired to teach. An opportunity for some faculty control in the new universities may have existed in the transitory period of the 1870s and 1880s, when the influence of religious denominations in higher education declined and such alternatives as secular wealth were beginning to appear. However, no alternative form of governance was sufficiently well known to serve as a model (the number of faculty trained in Europe, where such an alternative could have been observed, was still small at that time). Since faculty governance had not been practiced before, the legislatures which carried out the establishment of state universities and the wealthy individuals who endowed private universities chose the management model they knew best by vesting authority in an outside board and appointing a president to run the university on the board's behalf (the fact that the chief executive was given the same title as that of the head of a business corporation is in itself interesting). In a few instances the faculty urged that they should manage the affairs of the university. In 1878, Alexander Winchell stated that professors, rather than presidents or trustees, ought to have "the sole authority to expend the income of the university,"[10] and Joseph Jastrow of the University of Wisconsin urged a national meeting of university trustees in 1905 to relinquish their powers in favor of the faculty. In general, however, the faculty in the early American university felt no strong desire to manage their institutions. This lack of interest was reflected in a national poll conducted in 1912 which revealed that approximately 85 per cent of the faculty favored a greater degree of participation in university affairs but not control over the university. In rare cases in which the faculty did actively participate in several areas of university governance, such as in 1890 at Cornell University, the cause was not the faculty's struggle for power but rather the struggle between president and trustees, in which the faculty was used as a pawn.[11]

As early as 1876, the narrow responsibilities of the faculty were outlined by Daniel C. Gilman, the first president of Johns Hopkins University: "The faculty were not consulted in respect to investments. They did not fix the salaries nor the appropriations for the library and apparatus. In the construction of buildings their wishes were paramount, their advice indispensable; but the building contracts were in the hands, exclusively, of the trustees."[12] Harper of the University of Chicago, in his decennial report, stated a similar opinion: "It is a firmly established policy of the trustees that the responsibility for the settlement of educational questions rests with the faculties, and although in some instances the request of the faculty has not been granted for lack of the funds required, in no instance has the action of a faculty on educational questions been disapproved. It is clearly recognized that the trustees are responsible for the financial administration of the university but that to the faculties belongs in the fullest extent the care of the educational administration."[13]

These presidential declarations demonstrate that faculty participation in university governance was generally restricted to the area of educational matters. One reason may have been faculty unwillingness to cope with the additional responsibilities of administrative tasks. However, the important reason may have been the lack of professional security and therefore the relatively vulnerable position of the faculty during the first few decades of the American university. In the early university, the faculty did not differ much from their colleagues in the pre-Civil War college. Few of them had received any kind of advanced education and most of them were generalists who had to teach a variety of subjects. Thus they had little time to increase their knowledge; they were transmitters of knowledge rather than creators and transmitters of knowledge. Only in the 1870s and 1880s did university teaching as a career distinct from college teaching begin to emerge. By that time, a number of Americans had received their graduate training and their doctorates at German universities and had come back to teach, stressing graduate education.

The more advanced training of the faculty was undoubtedly a major reason for the increasing specialization which resulted in the separation of previous knowledge into the academic disciplines. This specialization led to the establishment of academic departments as the organizational setting for the new disciplines. The faculty ranks still used today were also a product of the 1890s. The major significance of the new rank system was that it laid the base for academic careers. Young scholars having completed their graduate studies were able to get full-time university teaching positions, a major innovation compared with the situation in the pre-Civil War college. A young man with a degree could serve as a tutor, but this was not a career position. Professors in the old college usually had to start their teaching careers after having spent many years in other occupations or professions, such as the ministry. Although the hierarchical rank system in the new university undoubtedly made university teaching more attractive as a career because of the inherent mobility it offered, it also created the inevitable antagonism between junior and senior faculty as well as between the latter and department chairmen. Nominally chosen from among the senior faculty to administer departments as first among equals, department chairmen at the turn of the century quite often ran their departments in a dictatorial manner and tended to regard them as their exclusive preserve.

The next step toward professionalization of the faculty career came with the introduction of tenure. Until 1906, the year the Carnegie retirement plan for professors was established, a teacher had no guarantee of a secure job. Only the introduction of tenure finally made it possible for the faculty as a group to claim the right to participate, without fear of reprisal, in some areas of governance. Limited faculty control over certain aspects of the educational program had existed in some of the early universities, but the faculty received the right of control only over the educational area in the first decade of the twentieth century. By that time, the battleground between faculty and university administration had shifted from control over educational matters to the issue of academic freedom. In the American university the faculty members were rather closely supervised by their governing boards, and academic freedom came to mean a faculty's right to a private life outside the university. This right was not safeguarded until well into the twentieth century. Most academic freedom cases involved political activities of faculty outside the campus, but some even dealt with the morality of professorial conduct outside the classroom. The long and continuous struggle for academic freedom eventually led the faculty to form the American Association of University Professors in 1915. The backing of this prestigious national association made it considerably easier for an accused faculty member to hold his own against the administration of his university.[14]

But collective actions by the faculty within a university helped them to go beyond defending their prerogatives and to force university administrations to let them participate in other areas of governance. Thus, in matters which affect the faculty of a university as a whole, the academic senate evolved into a rather strong institution on many campuses. Although the academic senate was not new as an institution, its influence went considerably beyond the merely consultative status it once had. It never became, however, a union which could engage in collective bargaining with the university administration and the governing board. The emergence of faculty unions may eventually lead to militant demands for participation in all governance areas if enough faculty accept the idea of collective bargaining, and the faculty senate could be designated as the faculty's bargaining agent.

As with the faculty of the early university, students had no power in decision-making. They were always regarded primarily as consumers of services produced by the other groups, and as consumers were never encouraged to show any interest in university governance, which might explain why demand for student participation in all areas of university governance appeared only recently. Students in the pre-Civil War college were pupils rather than students in the modern sense. Both their academic and their extracurricular activities were closely supervised by faculty and president. The old college could take its parental function seriously since it was usually very small and residential, which allowed faculty and president to know each student personally and to keep a close watch over his activities. The emergence of the new university brought about some relaxation of this supervision since the new institutions enrolled larger numbers of students. Students started to enjoy greater freedom but there was still no push for student participation in university governance.

The introduction of the elective principle in the later decades of the nineteenth century gave students an indirect opportunity to exercise some influence over their curriculum. The electives not only gave students a chance to take courses they were really interested in but also gave them an opportunity to vote with their feet by choosing some courses over others and thereby demonstrating their approval or disapproval of courses and teachers. The elective system was not, however, designed to give students a positive voice in the planning of their curriculum. A later timid step toward student participation in governance was the introduction of student government. Universities likely initiated this system for their own convenience rather than for the sake of students because it gave students conditional control over such areas as extracurricular activities and thus relieved the university administration of some tedious responsibilities. Honors rules extended the principle of student control over their activities into the classroom. However, both student government and honors rules represented only a slight increase in student participation in governance—students controlled only marginal areas, and the university administration had the right to revoke this control if it felt that students were unable to administer the system properly. The introduction of student evaluation of courses was the first step in the direction of effective student participation in the control of their curriculum. No data suggest, however, that faculty acceptance of student course evaluation necessarily led to an implementation of their demands.

Widespread student demand for effective participation in university governance was first visible on a nationwide scale during the 1968–1969 campus disorders. At some institutions, these disorders resulted in effective student participation in governance. At Columbia University, which had a long tradition of autocratic presidential rule and administrative authority, students are now sitting on policy-making committees. An even more important innovation that might eventually lead to full student participation in all areas of university governance is the election of students to the governing boards of some universities, such as the City University of New York.

The groups discussed so far share the common characteristic of being, or attempting to be, continuously part of the governance configuration. Outside regulatory agencies do not fit into this pattern because their constituencies are not limited to a single institution. These agencies are best described as silent partners in the context of university governance configurations since their function is to enforce certain minimum standards of quality, particularly in instruction.

The oldest regulatory bodies in the field of higher education were state governments. One of their traditional prerogatives is to accept or reject the charters of new institutions. Cornell University, for instance, barely had its charter approved by the New York State legislature. This control is a permanent prerogative of state governments and is used to force institutions that grant degrees to maintain certain minimum quality requirements; violations against the prescribed minimum standards can result in the revocation of a charter. Such a fate was unlikely for a university which maintained higher quality standards than those prescribed by state governments, but it did strike marginal colleges with insufficient facilities. The case of a small fundamentalist Bible college threatened with revocation of its charter by the New Jersey State Department of Education in 1969 shows that states do still take their power seriously. State governments also act as regulatory agencies when they allocate annual funds to state universities. These budgetary prerogatives enable legislatures to control at least the broad policies of state universities. In general, the large size and eminence of many state universities attest to the fact that legislatures have found it worthwhile to subsidize public higher education on a large scale.

The involvement of the federal government in public higher education goes back more than a century. The first Morrill Act (1862) probably led the way for the emergence of state universities as universities. This act set aside land revenues to support state colleges which taught agriculture and the mechanic arts, that is, state institutions which were willing to establish nonacademic, vocational programs. Although the act did not provide for direct control of the federal government over the land-grant institutions, it nevertheless specified that the land grants could be revoked if an institution failed to implement the conditions of the act. The more recent and more direct involvement of the federal government started when it began to allocate research funds and funds for student support and building projects. The second Morrill Act (1890), which provided for annual appropriations to land-grant universities by the federal government, is undoubtedly the forerunner of the present continuous and massive federal aid to higher education. Research contracts between federal agencies and universities have helped the schools to expand their research facilities and graduate programs considerably. Although many of these research projects were unrelated to instruction as such, they have indirectly benefited the quality of instruction by attracting high-caliber scholars, who in return attract the best students. The most comprehensive federal program aimed at increasing the quality of universities has been the establishment of "centers of excellence" at relatively small but promising universities. The government allocated substantial funds to permit these universities to become first-rank institutions.

Accrediting agencies now have a prominent place in American higher education. These agencies are a product of cooperation among universities, a phenomenon of the twentieth century. During the nineteenth century relations between institutions of higher education were competitive rather than cooperative, but gradually the necessity to cooperate emerged since universities faced many common issues. Out of this cooperation grew regional and special-interest associations which were given the right to accredit individual schools. Most colleges and universities were accredited by regional agencies, but special-interest associations followed a policy of accrediting departments or programs within a school. The accreditation process basically permitted a kind of self-regulation of colleges and universities. Of all special-interest associations which were able to gain control over professional programs offered by universities, the medical and legal professions are the most interesting since they were able to establish a monopoly (in the case of the medical profession) and a near monopoly (in the case of the legal profession) over the training of their prospective members. This control emerged gradually, once the new universities had assumed the responsibility for medical and legal training. Before the universities assumed this responsibility, medicine and law were taught in a wide variety of small professional schools. Their heterogeneity would have made it impossible for a professional association to control them effectively even if strong professional associations had existed at that time.

The governance configuration in the American university has changed considerably since the university grew from a rather small institution to a multiversity. Not only has the number of participants in the governance configuration increased considerably, but the relationship between the participants has changed as well. In the early American university of the post-Civil War years, the number of persons involved in governance was usually limited to two or three. In private universities established by wealthy individuals the governance configuration included the founder, the president, and the board of trustees. A distribution of prerogatives among these figures was certainly uncomplicated on paper, but the persons involved often aggressively attempted to increase their power. As a result, they were competitors rather than colleagues. In state universities the number of effective actors was only two: the legislature and the president. Governing boards of state universities seem to have been rather weak bodies at first.

The modern university operates under many internal and external constraints. The period of empire-building in higher education is mostly over, and the relationship among governing individuals has moved from one of competition toward one of cooperation. This change is a result not only of the increasing bureaucratization of the university but also of the increasing democratization within the institution. Although the modern university is still far from being a democratic organization in which decisions are based on equal representation of all groups within the university, the number of participants has nevertheless increased. Particularly important is the growing participation of faculty and students in university governance. The increasing number of constraints on the traditionally strong actors, such as the president and the governing board, is reflected in a system of checks and balances which renders it almost impossible for one person to make all major decisions alone. This fact is likely to prepare a base for either a university run in a truly representative manner or a new era of adversary factionalism in American university governance.

References

[1] Quoted in R. Hofstadter and W. Smith (Eds.), *American Higher Education—A Documentary History,* Vol. 2 (Chicago: University of Chicago Press, 1961), p. 781.

[2] C. Jencks and D. Riesman, *The Academic Revolution* (Garden City, N.Y.: Doubleday, 1968), p. 16.

[3] L. R. Veysey, *The Emergence of the American University* (Chicago: University of Chicago Press, 1965), p. 350.

[4] Hofstadter and Smith, *op. cit.,* pp. 774–775.
[5] *Ibid.,* p. 351.
[6] Veysey, *op. cit.,* p. 408.
[7] Hofstadter and Smith, *op. cit.,* p. 760.
[8] Veysey, *op. cit.,* p. 398.
[9] Hofstadter and Smith, *op. cit.,* p. 548.
[10] Quoted in Veysey, *op. cit.,* p. 392.
[11] *Ibid.,* p. 392.
[12] Hofstadter and Smith, *op. cit.,* p. 754.
[13] Quoted in *ibid.,* p. 775.
[14] Veysey, *op. cit.,* p. 416.

2

Rodney T. Hartnett

Trustee Power in America

In the spring of 1962, officers of the University of South Florida offered a teaching appointment, to begin the following fall, to a historian formerly on the staff of Vanderbilt University. After specific details regarding salary, courses to be taught, and class hours had been agreed upon (and after the would-be professor had visited the university community and purchased a house), the decision to employ the historian was reversed, primarily because of the opposition of the Florida State Board of Control (now the Board of Regents) to the professor's presumed political views.[1] In

December of 1965, thirty-three members of the faculty of St. John's University in New York were suspended, including twenty-two "without specific charges and hearings." These dismissals are particularly intriguing since those who sought the dismissals also had the legal authority to implement them, for the three top administrators of the institution (the president, the executive vice-president, and the vice-president for business affairs and treasurer of the university), were also president, vice-president, and secretary of the board, respectively.[2] In June of 1967, a letter of intent to grant tenure to an assistant professor of political science at the University of Hawaii was revoked by the administration. Subsequently, a committee of the University of Hawaii Faculty Senate found that the cause offered for revocation was not justified, and recommended to the Board of Regents that the revocation be rescinded. The Board of Regents, however, rejected the Senate committee report and supported the revocation of the letter of intent.[3] Finally, in September 1969, the Board of Regents of the University of California ordered that dismissal proceedings be initiated for an acting assistant professor of philosophy at UCLA who publicly acknowledged membership in the Communist Party.[4] In June 1970, the professor was fired.

These are not isolated cases, turned up with great difficulty after considerable searching and probing. Rather, these cases are only four chosen from hundreds that could be cited as apparent evidence of trustee power in American higher education. Each suggests that the trustees, by the authority vested in them in their institutions' charters, had a great deal of influence over the operation of the institutions. But do trustees, in general, have much power in American higher education? Should they?

From the frequent use of the word *power* in discussions of academic governance, one would be tempted to conclude that the word has fairly uniform meaning for its users. Likewise, such words as *authority, control,* and *influence*—which occur quite frequently in discussions of power in academia—might be assumed to be referring to quite specific behaviors or arrangements among people. In fact, however, considerable confusion exists among these concepts, not only among those who employ such terms in informal discussions of who runs the university, but also among sociologists who have made it their business to study the meaning of such concepts.[5]

Perhaps the most frequent misunderstanding occurs over the notions of power and authority. As used in this chapter, the terms have different—and quite explicit—meanings. Power, as set forth by McGrath (see Chapter Twelve), refers to the ability, of individuals or groups, to control the policy-making processes in the academic community. Influence seems to differ from power in that influence connotes informal procedures in contrast to formal ones, and persuasion as opposed to simply giving orders. Although theoretically this distinction may be an important one, in this chapter the concepts are treated as though they are synonymous. The trustees who wield considerable influence over the affairs of an institution, in this context, are regarded as having substantial *power*. Power needs no institutional sanction.

Authority, on the other hand, refers to power vested in an office or role (that is, "authorized" or institutionally recognized power). Thus, authority might be viewed as *limited* power relegated to certain roles. A department chairman, for example, can often force a faculty member to teach a course, even when the faculty member is opposed to such an assignment, because such a requirement is generally regarded as "legitimate," that is, within the limits of the chairman's authority. The same department chairman, however, might have a more difficult time forcing a faculty member to assign a certain percentage of letter grades to students in his course, since in this instance the legitimacy of such a requirement is highly questionable. The chairman's authority, in other words, is limited and restricted. Power, on the other hand, knows no such limits. If the aforementioned department chairman were successful in obtaining a prescribed grade distribution from the faculty member, his *power*—at least over that faculty member—would be considerable, even though his authority might be insignificant.

This last point implies that power over one person (or of one group over another) does not necessarily mean that the power is generalizable to others. This idea deserves elaboration. One of the most common misconceptions of power has treated power as if it were only an attribute of a person (say, president or dean) or group (trustees or faculty). Such a conception inevitably leads to the question, "Who are the power holders?" This question is vacant unless one also asks "Over whom?" It is well known that in certain situations person X may dominate Y, while being subservient in relations with Z. This is also true of groups. To quote Richard Emerson, "In making these necessary qualifications we force ourselves to face up to the obvious—power is a property of the social relation; it is not an attribute of the actor."[6] Thus, in discussing trustees power, the questions "Do trustees hold the power?" and "Should trustees hold the power?" are to some extent meaningless. We will probably be spinning wheels until we ask, instead, "In what situations do trustees exhibit power? Power over whom?"

Kenneth Boulding has indicated that many of the problems of urban America remain unsolved because the people who have the power and authority to run the cities live not in the cities but "somewhere outside."[7] Boulding's analysis of what's wrong with our cities has its parallel, some feel, in the way colleges and universities are governed in America.

Before we move to a discussion of trustee power, let us first consider who the trustees are. A great deal of information about trustees' backgrounds and educational attitudes is available.[8] Trustees, as a group, are quite wealthy. More than half have annual incomes exceeding $30,000, and at private universities 49 per cent have an annual income of $75,000 or more. Many are business executives. At private universities, for example, nearly half are executives of manufacturing, merchandising, or investment firms. The overwhelming majority are male, white, Protestant, and in their fifties and sixties. Politically, they tend to regard themselves as moderate Republicans. In 1968 approximately two-thirds of them said their political and social views were similar to those of Richard Nixon and Nelson Rockefeller. Although there is some evidence of changes in the composition of many governing boards since 1968—particularly in the direction of including more women, blacks, and people under forty—the preceding statements would still hold up as quite accurate, general descriptions of American college and university trustees in 1970.[9]

How did most of these people become trustees? It depends on the type of institution. At private institutions, many of them—usually over half—are appointed by trustees already serving on the board, and the rest are usually elected by alumni or appointed by a religious group. At public institutions, most of them are either appointed by the governor or elected by the public. In any event, once they become board members they, along with the other trustees serving on the board, form the controlling corporate entity. It is not just that they are the ultimate governing body; more importantly, they are the corporation.

What are their views about authority in higher education? How do they think power should be distributed? One of the complaints made most frequently by disenchanted members of the academic community is that the wrong people are making the decisions. In a survey of faculty opinion regarding participation in academic decision-making at one institution, for example, 51 per cent of the faculty included in the survey felt that "the faculty has too little influence on decisions; more of the decision-making power should rest with the faculty," and most of them indicated that they were either dissatisfied or very dissatisfied with this situation.[10] Such sentiments are probably characteristic of faculty and student groups on most campuses, the feeling being, of course, that it is the administrators and trustees who are making the decisions. But how do the trustees feel about their role (and the roles of others) in campus decision-making?

According to recent data,[11] trustees tend to favor a hierarchical system in which decisions are made at the top and passed "down." For example, over 50 per cent of the total sample of trustees believe that faculty and students should *not* have major authority in eight of sixteen typical campus decisions. The proportion feeling that trustees or administrators alone should have major authority in making the decision exceeds 40 per cent in twelve of the sixteen decisions. Some of these are particularly interesting. For example, 63 per cent say that the appointment of an academic dean should be made with only the administrators and trustees having major authority; or, to say it another way, 63 per cent feel that the faculty should *not* have major authority in the appointment of their dean. Similarly, 57 per cent would exempt the faculty from major authority in the awarding of honorary degrees; 58 per cent would exempt them from major authority in policies regarding faculty leaves. To many, of course, these findings come as no surprise. But, surprising or not, they do help underscore some of the very wide differences of opinion among members of the academic community as to who should govern.

Second, there is a perceptible difference in the kinds of decisions for which trustees feel other groups should and should not have substantial authority. For example, they feel that faculty authority should be greatest in academic matters, such as whether to add or delete specific courses, or what criteria should be employed in admitting students. Student authority is judged relevant in matters of student life, such as housing, cheating, fraternities and sororities, and the like.

Third, though the trustees generally prefer an arrangement in which the faculty and students do not have major authority, neither do they want to "rule" by themselves. Generally, they prefer major authority for decisions, except for presidential appointments, to rest with the administration alone or with the administration and trustees jointly. Thus, the "top down" model must be modified. Trustees prefer their decision-making ability to be singularly authoritative only when it comes to choosing the president. Having selected him, however, they like to lean heavily on him (and his administrative colleagues) for making the decisions.

Naturally, there is a great deal of variation on these matters among types of institutions. Trustees of selective private institutions seem most inclined to include other members of the academic community in the decision-making process, while trustees of nonselective public institutions are more inclined toward a power-at-the-top arrangement. At public junior colleges, 50 per cent or more of the trustees feel that administrators and trustees alone should have major authority in deciding thirteen of the sixteen issues, but at selective private institutions, they hold out for only four. The concept of democratic governance or shared authority clearly has a more receptive audience among trustees at private institutions. In fact, ordering institutions according to the trustees' belief in shared authority would correspond very closely to an ordering of institutional types by educational prestige—that is, where prestige is defined by the usual (but not necessarily reasonable) indices of student ability, faculty prominence, and the like. With the exception of the selective public universities, division on this question occurs according to whether institutions are public or private. Thus, in terms of their views regarding authority, trustees generally seem to prefer a hierarchical arrangement or system of graded authority, but the diversity in these orientations across different types of institutions is very large. It makes little sense, therefore, to talk about trustee power as if it were uniform throughout American higher education.

Before we move into a discussion of power, let us compare the American system of trusteeships with the English system. Although it is true that in England also the lay-dominated boards (courts and councils) are the ultimate governing bodies (except for Oxford and Cambridge, whose constitutions involve almost complete control by their academic members), there are nonetheless several very basic differences between the systems of governance in the two countries, differences worth clarifying since they have relevance for any consideration of trustee power.

First, there is the matter of board composition. Although the British boards are lay-dominated, between one-fourth and one-third of their members are members of the faculty. In the United States faculty representation on governing boards is closer to 1 or 2 per cent. Furthermore, unlike their American counterparts, the laymen serving on the boards of British universities generally are not men of wealth, but instead represent a broad range of educational backgrounds, occupations, and skills. Of course, as in the United States, there is in Britain faculty criticism of the predominance of lay members on governing boards. More important, however, is the fact that in Britain, the legal corporation consists of the officers, faculty, administration, and student body. They, in effect, are the "owners" of the institution. In America, as already indicated, the opposite is true. The trustees form the corporation, and the members of the administration and faculty, legally, are their "employees."

This is not merely an important legal distinction; it has

even more pronounced practical implications. Board members in Britain have very little influence on the affairs of the institution. Situations in America such as those described in the introductory paragraphs of this chapter are viewed with astonishment and dismay among British educators. Even most of the business conducted at board meetings is dominated by members of the faculty, even though they compose, as stated earlier, a minority of the board. In fact, except for certain business matters, much of what the British boards decide must meet the approval of the faculty senate.

It is important to remember that all of British higher education is public. There are no private institutions of higher education, as we know them, in Britain (the colleges of Cambridge and Oxford being special cases). More than 85 per cent of all university finance comes from public sources.[12] Thus, at least in terms of board composition, it might be more meaningful to compare the British system with the public sector in America. In any event, while there are similarities between the systems of governance in these two countries, the differences are great, and worth keeping in mind as we consider the role of trustees and the concept of power. It would appear that the major role played by trustees in England is one of advisor or interpreter of the public interest.

Having defined the meaning of power, described the predominant characteristics of trustees and their attitudes about authority, and compared the American and British trusteeships, we are now ready to turn to the central question: What is the nature and extent of the power of trustees in American higher education? As we have already seen, power does not necessarily follow authority. It is generally agreed, among almost all who are familiar with higher education in Britain, that the boards have much legal authority but very little power. There is less agreement on this question in America. In discussing the power of trustees, McGrath (in Chapter Twelve), says: "In principle the trustees have much. In actuality, in the setting of the policies which determine an institution's essential character, they either have little power, or choose not to exercise it." This view has many supporters. In writing about the role of trustees, John Corson suggests that, in spite of their broad authority, trustees find themselves "unable to influence decisions that determine the basic character of the institution."[13]

Clark Kerr points out that "there are more claimants for power than ever before, and there is no more power to be divided. Someone must lose if others gain—a zero-sum game."[14] He then suggests that, in general, there is less power and influence on the campus, since the major gains in the quest for academic power have been made by the federal government (which now supplies one-fourth of all funds spent by institutions of higher learning). "On campus, the big losers, particularly in domination of the budget, have been the board and the president. Their best instrument of control is now shared with others."[15] Who have been the "big gainers" on campus? In Kerr's opinion, it is the students: "There are more of them; they are more activist; they have more grievances against the campus and against society; and they are already making gains, and they may make more. . . . On campus the students are the new men of power."[16]

There are others who feel that the trustees have a great deal of power and can cite much evidence for this position. If we again consider the cases described in the opening paragraph of this chapter, in fact, it seems somewhat naive to argue very convincingly against the idea of *some* trustee power. How much power, and in what situations, no doubt depends on various historical and organizational features of the institution. At church-related institutions, for example, we might expect to find more trustee power than in independent or public institutions. The previously mentioned situation at St. John's, where the officers of the institution were also officers of the board, serves as a good example of this. Even here, however, how much power the trustees wield depends on the situation, the groups involved, and the eventual outcome. It would appear, in this case, that the trustees had not only the authority, but the power as well, for in spite of faculty attempts to protest the dismissals through weeks of picketing, striking, and other forms of pressure, their efforts in the long run were apparently to no avail. Within two years of the original strife at St. John's, almost every faculty member who had been openly opposed to the conditions of government at the university had either left or become silent.

Let us consider another case of competition for power. At New Jersey's Trenton State College, in the fall of 1969, the faculty demanded the resignation of their president, who had held the office for only one year. (There is disagreement regarding the reasons for the faculty ire but they are irrelevant for the point being made here.) The trustees held a series of hearings, considered the case against the president, and then exonerated him from the faculty charges and extended to him a vote of confidence. Thus, the trustees, through their vested authority, had made a crucial decision which, if it held up, would have been evidence of power. But the story does not end there. The faculty continued to put pressure on the president and the board with tactics, interestingly enough, that were not too different from those employed at St. John's several years earlier—picket lines, petitions, support of student groups, and the like. In February of 1970 the president resigned.

In the St. John's case the trustees appear to have authority and power. In the Trenton State instance the trustees had the authority, but their attempt to use it was not successful. Instead, the faculty, who had no legal authority in this matter, held the power. They, not the trustees, had the ability to shape the nature of the institution.

Why this difference? Why were the authority holders able to seize the power at St. John's but not at Trenton State? There is no single or simple answer, of course. Many institutional variables come into play. The most crucial difference, however, seems to hinge on the question of *relevant support*. It would appear that to defy authority, strong, relevant support is a necessary condition. The Trenton State faculty had it; the St. John's group did not. We note that "the general faculty of St. John's showed a high degree of apathy and a reluctance openly to support action looking toward improvement of the state of government at the university" and "although faculty activists often claimed faculty support, the evidence suggests they had extreme difficulty in arousing any massive faculty involvement in the issues they were raising."[17] At Trenton State, on the other hand, approximately 80 per cent of the faculty and administrators expressed no confidence in the president, and supported the push for his resignation. Furthermore, the three faculty organizations—Faculty Association, local AAUP, and Faculty Senate—supported the move, and the presidents of these three organizations assumed leadership roles.

To emphasize further the importance of support for those seeking power without authority, consider an instance of student protest which was not successful. At the University of Chicago, a group of students took over the administration building in protest of the institution's refusal to renew the contract of a nontenured faculty member. After several days of sitting in without evidence of capitulation from the administration, the student group left the building and normal activities resumed. Although it is true that this student group failed to achieve their goal partially because of a firm, unyielding administrative response, the more important reason was the students' failure to obtain the necessary student and faculty support.

Thus, in the quest of power in the academy, the basic ground rules appear to be not too different from those that apply to community power, political power, or any other kind of power: to the extent that the group can marshal substantial, relevant support for its cause, its chances of success are increased, whether it has authority or not.

The adjective *relevant* is an important modifier when one speaks of support. The support, if it is to be effective, must come from those who are in positions to exert pressure that will be felt. In the case of a faculty cause, for example, support which comes from a radical faculty group on some other campus is not likely to be very effective. What kind of support is relevant depends on the situation.

The questions, "Who holds the power?" and "How much power?" are too simplistic. No one group really "holds" the power or even a certain portion of it. Power is situation-dependent. The allocation of the power in certain situations depends on which group can marshal support for its position. The person or group with authority (which is not synonymous with power) usually has a tactical advantage in jockeying for power, but authority alone is never sufficient in the face of substantial, relevant opposition. Even the question "Who had the power in that specific situation?" often cannot be answered for a long time, for often the final settlement of a crisis or disagreement is not clear for many months.

It seems equally naive to ask "Who *should* have the power?" Since situations vary from campus to campus and even on the same campus over time, power is inevitably elusive. A more reasonable question might be "Should *anyone* hold the power?" Clark Kerr makes a cogent point in this regard:

> *Attempted solutions on the basis of ideology—all power to the faculty or all power to the students or all power to the regents who represent the people—are fraught with danger. There can be no clear preference for one solution versus another solution on principle, given the nature of the academic institution; and ideological solutions tend to be absolutist, authoritarian, and across-the-board in a situation that calls for tolerance, a large measure of individual freedom, and the precise fitting of governance to special situations. Attempted solutions on the basis of power alone—on who has the money or the votes or mob pressure—can tear a campus apart, and once torn apart it is hard to put together again.*[18]

Nevertheless, in spite of every attempt to employ policies of democratic governance and to proceed by consensus, occasional conflicts are almost certain to develop. Even with the best of intentions, reason is not always possible when concerned people meet to consider alternative points of view. In such situations, competition for power is almost inevitable. Who gets the power depends on many things. It might appear that as a general rule, the trustees, who legally have a great deal of authority and access to sources of money, are in a good position to assume much power as well. But the federal government, the faculty, the administration, the students, the alumni, and others all have their own sources of power. In general, it would seem, as Kerr suggested, that relative to the power of several of these other claimants, the trustees' power is on the wane. But in specific situations at specific institutions, their power may still be considerable, depending on the support of these other groups to muster substantial relevant support for a dissenting point of view.

References

[1] "Academic Freedom and Tenure: The University of South Florida," *AAUP Bulletin,* March 1964, pp. 44–57.

[2] "College and University Government: St. John's University," *AAUP Bulletin,* September 1968, pp. 325–361.

[3] "Academic Freedom and Tenure: University of Hawaii," *AAUP Bulletin,* March 1969, pp. 29–40.

[4] "UCLA Told to Fire Communist Teacher," *Chronicle of Higher Education,* September 29, 1969, p. 6.

[5] As just one example of this, see the Communications by Butler and Harrison in "On Power and Authority: An Exchange on Concepts," *American Sociological Review,* October 1960, pp. 731–732.

[6] R. Emerson, "Power-Dependence Relations," *American Sociological Review,* February 1962, pp. 31–41.

[7] K. Boulding, "What Can We Know and Teach about Social Systems?" *Social Science Education Consortium Newsletter,* June 1968, p. 3.

[8] See R. Hartnett, *College and University Trustees: Their Backgrounds, Roles, and Educational Attitudes* (Princeton, N.J.: Educational Testing Service, 1969). M. Rauh's book, *The Trusteeship of Colleges and Universities* (New York: McGraw-Hill, 1969) was also based, to a large extent, on this national survey, which was conducted during the spring of 1968.

[9] For a detailed account of these changes and some speculations about their meaning for the future, see R. Hartnett, *The New College Trustees: Some Predictions for the 1970s* (Princeton, N.J.: Educational Testing Service, 1970).

[10] A. Dykes, *Faculty Participation in Academic Decision-Making* (Washington, D.C.: American Council on Education, 1968).

[11] These paragraphs borrow rather heavily from Hartnett (1969), *op. cit.*

[12] *Higher Education.* Report of the Committee appointed by the Prime Minister under the chairmanship of Lord Robbins, 1961–1963 (London: Her Majesty's Stationery Office, 1965).

[13] J. Corson, *Governance of Colleges and Universities* (New York: McGraw-Hill, 1960), p. 49.

[14] C. Kerr, "Governance and Functions," *Daedalus,* Winter 1970, p. 107.

[15] *Ibid.,* p. 112.

[16] *Ibid.*

[17] "College and University Government: St. John's University," *op. cit.,* p. 330.

[18] Kerr, *op. cit.,* p. 119.

3

L. Richard Meeth

Administration and Leadership

In his inaugral address as president of Harvard in 1869, Charles W. Eliot remarked, "The only conceivable aim of a college government in our days is to broaden, deepen, and invigorate American teaching in all branches of learning." The central and underlying purpose of this whole volume is essentially to improve the teaching-learning process and product; this chapter focuses on the dysfunctional elements that administrative-faculty relationships generate. Because these elements interfere with good teaching and effective learning, several alternative structures for improved relationships are proposed.

Several assumptions underlie the major arguments and organizational patterns proposed. First, the collegial structure for the faculty is more beneficial to them and more appropriate for an institution than is a union or a straight employer-employee relationship. Howe discusses this viewpoint fully in Chapter Eight. It is stated here only as an assumption. The collegial structure has been a very effective way of preserving the partnership between professionals and laymen. This partnership, unique to American higher education, has produced great diversity and correspondingly great strength in our system, along with an adequate system of checks and balances.

Second, whether the board, president, or others make the changes in collegiate administrative structure is not as important as it is to recognize that changes have already taken place within the college and that they must be acted upon or considered in academic decision-making. Although the board and president can most easily inaugurate changes in the power structure, the most successful changes take into account what is happening outside the college.

Third, if administrative officers do not want a faculty union, they have to adjust the traditional forms of college administration. Unionism in both faculty and student groups is rapidly growing at all levels of education in the United States, and higher education will not be an exception unless the structures bend or yield great amounts of authority, information, and exclusivity.

Fourth, fault or blame for the dysfunctional elements in the relationship between administrators and faculty cannot be placed at either door. Personality quirks, ignorance, communication breakdowns, structural complexities, and external pressures all contribute to the breach between faculty and administration. Perhaps the single most important cause is that the breach has become a self-fulfilling prophecy. Both parties have long attributed much more to the gulf between faculty and administration than it rightly deserved, causing the gulf to attract widespread interest and raising each new generation on the foibles and stupidity of the other side, so that the crack has widened in a self-perpetuating process. Although the role of managers and the style of management in American higher education have changed radically since World War II, the relationship with faculty has changed very little. Faculties have not kept pace organizationally either. This organizational, perhaps even cultural, lag makes the question of relationship between the administration and the faculty critical. Add to these factors the pressure from students for relevant teaching and learning, and the possibility of total breakdown or revolutionary change immediately looms large.

This critical dilemma, focusing as it does on the tremendous changes in the role and practice of management, prompts a review of those basic changes which have been of particular significance to the relationships with faculty.[1] The first is the shift from secrecy to publicity in the general conduct of administrative and academic affairs. The collection and dissemination of detailed information about the operation of institutions of higher learning make trustees, state and federal officials, and the community at large much more aware than they were in the past of the way in which a college is operated. Traditionally academic administrators were secret agents of the college, but the trend now is toward an open style of administration. "This has been true with respect both to the disclosure of information to the outside world and to the modification or elimination of some of the traditional 'information screens' that have existed within the academic community."[2] This development in college and university administration is a result not only of increased pressures from federal and state government, foundations, and other agencies for information about the operation of each institution but also, particularly with the advent of the computer, of the many efficient ways which have been designed for gathering and disseminating information. As colleges have come to know more about themselves, they have also tended to share that information considerably more than they did in the past.

The open dissemination of information on the organization and management of an institution bears greatly upon administrative relationships with faculty. Generally it is a great asset; faculty are informed about priorities of the administration and about functionings within their own and other departments and have a potentially better understanding of the college budget and of reasons why expenditures can or cannot be made in a given year for a given program. On the other hand, indiscriminate distribution of information can lead to very hard feelings among departments, particularly when one gets a larger share of each dollar than another which feels equally deserving. Jealousies and insecurities can grow because some departments have a large number of majors and others do not. Managers need to take particular care to reckon with the truth inherent in the maxim "a little learning is a dangerous thing." Quite often a presentation of the budget to faculty members who do not understand the budget process leads to greater dysfunction rather than to the desired increase in communication. Thus, although openness is a fact in college management, managers can make it an asset or a liability in relationships with faculty.

The second major shift in management is the development, sometimes formal and sometimes informal, of a cabinet style of government in place of the presidential system of executive leadership traditional in American higher education. Increasingly the task of managing internal college and university affairs has been delegated to an assortment of vice-presidents, deans, business managers, and directors. Ordinarily these second line officers meet with the president either formally as an administrative council or informally as a kitchen cabinet to discuss major institutional policies and decisions. Frequently the president permits the members of the cabinet to vote but in other instances he listens to their advice and makes the final decisions himself. Rourke and Brooks comment upon this style of university management:

> *The emergence of the cabinet system of government in university administration simply reflects the necessities imposed by size and complexity. The president becomes a prime minister because he no longer can administer the university alone. Management of business firms went through a somewhat similar process earlier in this country, as in the course of time business firms moved out from the control of individual freewheeling entrepreneurs into the jurisdiction of executive committees. In spite of the long-standing tendency in organization theory to disparage such plural executive arrangements, universities like other organizations have*

found it necessary when they reached an advanced stage to establish systems of governance in which the chief executive shares authority over decision-making with other officials. The range of subjects over which decisions must now range is so vast as to demand the advantages of division of labor in the performance of the executive function as well as in the other tasks of large organizations.[3]

Again, whether decentralization of authority aids effective relationships with the faculty is a moot point. Cabinet government can cut off the president or the deans from faculty by increasing the power base and forming a solid administrative front as much as it can be an effective means for efficient administration of faculty policies and decisions. The president can lose direct access to the faculty and lesser administrators can gain direct access to the trustees; both these changes have been generally harmful in higher education administration in the past. Whether or not cabinet governance is helpful to the faculty, it is a clear-cut direction of the future. There have been many proposals for decentralizing administrative responsibility in the last few years but not a single one for centralizing responsibility.

The third change is the development and utilization of new forms of decision-making which generally are less subjective than the styles of the past. The development of administrative theory in higher education, its concomitant decision-making models, and the growth of data production relating to college and university management have combined to increase the flow of routine decision-making and to relieve to some extent the pressures upon central administrators, who in the past had to concentrate most of their energy on routine rather than on critical nonreoccurring decisions. Routinizing much administrative decision-making has allowed major administrators to concentrate their energies on long range plans, formulation of institutional goals, and implementation of these goals in new programs and designs.

This efficient decision-making process tends to leave faculty out. As administrative energies focus upon goals and long range plans, the direction and tone of an institution tend to be set without the faculty's ever being aware of what is happening. Routine decisions in the aggregate often are a more critical revelation of faculty-administrative relationships than are the nonreoccurring decisions, which have generally involved forethought and political maneuvering among faculty and administrators. Thus while increasingly effective decision-making processes can increase the time available for administrators to spend with faculty in major decision-making, they can also be a means for bypassing the faculty.

The fourth major shift has been from a job/task-oriented administrative structure to a person-centered process. Sensitivity training and encounter groups are superseding time and motion studies as primary devices for improving management. The person performing a task has become more important to productivity than efficient procedure as decision-making becomes a matter more of who participates than of the content or magnitude of the decision. The effect of Dewey, James, Freud, Jung, and Rogers can be felt at every level of college administration.

Person-centered administration can leave out faculty as effectively as task-oriented administration can. Including too few or too many persons produces the same result—a breakdown in effective decision-making. Becoming sensitive to faculty members may result in a renewed paternalism or a failure to act against their wishes, either of which makes them less than equals. Again, the management tool is no better or worse than the managers who employ it.

The fifth and perhaps most important management change is the creation of multicampus networks or consortia in many states and regions. These new multiple administrative units have generated new problems as higher education seeks to adjust to the demands of the last quarter of the twentieth century and the advent of the twenty-first. In large systems with some form of central administration, faculty and administrators lose a measure of autonomy and consequent responsibility for and interest in programs on their own campuses. Multiple campus systems and consortia can of course provide many benefits which an individual college or campus cannot possibly afford, but the dangers are ever present that the system competes with its constituents and that responsibility and control shift from the member institutions to the central administration.

Thus once more, as in the other four management changes, there is a tendency to increase central control and an enhanced possibility for leaving the faculty further behind and in the dark than they now are. At the same time management techniques and innovations open the door for concrete means of sharing with faculty and students the governance of American colleges and universities. The key lies in the role of the manager who is most responsible for this relationship, commonly the dean.

The dean is the man in the middle. He is known variously as vice-president for academic affairs, provost, chancellor, dean of the college, or dean of the faculty. Commonly he is appointed by the president from the faculty to relate administrative and faculty policy and procedure. He has been called a "prophet, prime mover, keeper of the status quo, skull collector, servant of the faculty, trail-blazer, weather vane, builder, housekeeper, maverick, and lackey."[4] But in the simplest vernacular he is the man with two hats but hopefully not two heads. The dean must balance necessary faculty authority and desirable administrative efficiency. Understanding this paradox is crucial to understanding his role. Earl McGrath's concept of the role of the academic dean returns to the central point of this chapter:

> *The academic commonwealth ought not to be a loose federation of quasi-autonomous subject matter principalities but rather a cohesive society in which community interests prevail over individual. The dean by position, perspective, and responsibility should be the person qualified to represent and articulate these overriding interests. If he rejects these responsibilities and, as is more and more the case, the president cannot assume them, it is hard to see how the institution can have any clear sense of mission and the education of its students any commonality of purpose or substance.*[5]

Changes in the role of the dean since World War II have been as revolutionary as have other changes in management. There has been a strong progression from "almost sole concern with students (in the days before student deans existed), through a phase when students and the curriculum were his largest responsibility, to a period when curriculum and faculty demanded the greatest part of his energies, finally [to] a place where his major concern is the faculty alone."[6] Through this period the dean has moved from being primarily assistant to the president for student affairs to being man in the middle. This shift is deplored by many deans, yet it has unmistakably taken place and without conscious effort. At least four distinct concepts of the role the dean plays in relating the administration to the faculty have emerged in the literature and in the life styles of men who have occupied the position.

The first role is that of the autocrat who regards faculty as employees rather than partners. He is the assistant to the president for the faculty and holds the power and the responsibility firmly in his own hands. With the power granted him by the president he acts independently of faculty wishes, extending administrative authority into faculty matters. By position he is the head of the faculty, but he should not be considered the leader of the faculty since leadership implies a following. The autocratic dean generally places efficiency before effectiveness and acts as a politician when he works with the faculty. The big question posed by the autocratic dean model is whether efficiency in college government is worth the disruption of faculty traditions and freedom. For short periods of time the answer may be yes, but, in the long run, the autocratic dean has little to commend him as far as improving relationships between the administration and the faculty. Probably fewer deans than presidents play the autocratic role in college administration, but still a large number operate in this fashion, particularly in smaller institutions.

Servant of the faculty is the second possible role for college deans today. The faculty servant usually emerges from the faculty, holds a faculty viewpoint quite often to the exclusion of an administrative point of view, and considers himself the chief lobbyist for the faculty before the president and board of trustees. He sees his primary mission as preserving the status quo, which, given most faculties in American colleges, means the preservation of a conservative position. The big question with this role is whether faculty-administrative harmony and peace are gained at the price of institutional progress or survival. Change is very difficult to achieve in an institution under the deanship of a faculty servant.

The third alternative is that of academic leader. It is in theory an independent position in which the dean thinks for himself yet recognizes his dependence upon support from both the president and the faculty. "Leadership is a process of mutual stimulation—[a] social interactional phenomenon in which the attitudes, ideals, and aspirations of the followers play as important a determining role as do the individuality and personality of the leader."[7] Most of the recent literature concerning the academic deanship and administrative theory in general stresses the academic leader as the ideal role for an administrator.

Since leadership is as much given to a person as it is acquired by him, the role remains highly personality-centered and may change depending upon the issues under discussion. Although the role is theoretically and ideally sound, the big question is whether it can ever exist long enough to transform an institution or improve faculty-administrative relationships. Since so much burden is placed upon the personality of the individual dean, it is doubtful that any man could long be an academic leader in the day-to-day, routine operation and decision-making which are necessary in an institution.

The fourth role—the dean as change agent—has been creeping up on the profession for some time and is probably the most viable one in present college administration. Because of the pressures upon college administrators from students and faculty, the role of academic leader is virtually impossible since it requires acquiescence from faculty and students. And the role of faculty servant often results in extensive compromise. When Gould studied the academic deanship in 1963, both he and McGrath decried the direction in which the deans at that time were moving. McGrath said:

> *Very few deans expressed the view that the occupant of the office should be a serious and continuous student of the ends and means of higher education in a rapidly changing social*

> *order. Fewer still seem to believe that the dean ought to have a clear and comprehensive view of the goals toward which the institution over which he presides should be moving and the ways in which its total resources should be used to reach its objectives. Some appear to feel that to have a clear view of institutional purposes and to urge their realization through specific policies related to the curriculum and the faculty would be tantamount to undemocratic if not tyrannical administration. These views of the dean's functions seem peculiarly unfortunate at this moment in our national history.*[8]

Possibly academic deans have not accepted the role of leader precisely because they have not known either how to lead or in what direction to go. As a change agent, however, a dean can play a catalytic role in achieving harmony within the faculty and the administration and at the same time can exercise some direction over the movement of the institution toward specific and clear-cut goals devised through long range planning. The change agent role is a combination of the best of the faculty servant and the academic leader roles. The change agent dean stimulates the leadership potential which resides within the faculty as the fundamental source of academic authority and does not overtly pull or push toward objectives he has determined. He identifies problems of critical importance to the institution but does not take action apart from the will of the president and the faculty.[9]

As change agent the dean must be wise as a serpent yet gentle as a lamb. At times he must act as an autocrat; at other times he must appear to abdicate the leadership role entirely in favor of faculty consensus. He must know how to plant ideas and make them appear to be the insights of others. He must capitalize upon the ideas of others which help to move the institution toward its goals. His most effective avenue as change agent is in selection of personnel and materials, which is a considerably more objective and less personality-oriented task than most of the role activities just cited. He is able to change the institution by, in descending order of importance, appointing new faculty, setting student admissions criteria and programs, making administrative appointments, establishing and maintaining curricular requirements, and selecting books for the college library.

Fundamentally this role differs from that of academic leader in that the change agent never moves beyond the point to which the faculty is able to go, whereas the leader may go far beyond even the comprehension of the faculty or the administration as long as he maintains the charismatic acceptance of his followers. Essentially the change agent is behind the scenes, the academic leader is out in front. He works through the faculty and administration rather than with the faculty and administration or, in the case of the servant, for the faculty. Although he shares the same goals as the academic leader, he pushes rather than pulls, and his role does not depend nearly so much upon acceptance by faculty or administration. The role of change agent is the only one that leads neither to confrontation with the faculty or with the administration nor to a takeover in the government of the institution by either group. Perhaps the best way to describe the precarious yet essential position of the change agent dean is to call him the balance wheel of institutional movement.

The unwillingness of deans to assume any strong role in the past has been a large factor in the denigration of administration by faculty. In the absence of administrative leadership many faculties assumed responsibilities which they were ill equipped and unprepared to maintain. Having assumed them, however, they were reluctant to relinquish them or found that they could not handle them effectively and readily gave them to poor administrators to perform in their behalf. If academic deans refuse to accept the role of change agent, they may well see themselves replaced entirely by a different kind of administrator. They may once again be either servants of the faculty or assistants to the president. In fact, the same institution may find itself with both persons if unionism continues to increase.

If the role of the dean is to be that of change agent, how then should the administration be organized to support this role most effectively? With the new roles of management and the managerial revolution, the best organization of the college administration is not yet clear. Few illustrations can be pointed to as working models, but the best structure must meet several criteria: The structure must be so designed that it can handle conflict within itself; the organization must be flexible, not rigid; open-ended, not closed; dynamic, not static. The structure must allow all positions to be heard and communication to flow openly and freely at all levels. The structure must provide rewards, not only long range job satisfactions but also immediate rewards such as promotion and adequate salary increases. The structure must give faculty and administrators a sense of belonging to the institution and of supporting the purposes which the institution espouses. The structure must regard individuals as members of a group and not treat any individuals as special or beyond the dictates of the group. The structure must be able to forgive failure by its design and open-ended nature; it must recognize that failure does occur and when forgiven produces a stronger organization than when castigated.

Historically the structure of American higher education administration has not been based upon any theoretical criteria or group dynamics principles. It has grown out of necessity and imitation of the form of other institutions without necessarily possessing their needs. Three common patterns of relationship within the administration have developed since the 1920s. Robert Merry categorizes them in this way: the inside-outside pattern, in which the dean is responsible for internal affairs, the president for external; the duo, in which the dean is the representative of the president and there is a sharing of responsibilities; and the trio or quartet (usually found in small institutions), in which the dean and the president work very closely with the business manager or the vice-president for development or both.[10] Some of the new arrangements proposed in this chapter fall into one of the three traditional patterns and others go beyond to suggest possibly a fourth and a fifth general pattern for the future.

The first possible method of organizing the administration to enhance relationships with the faculty is to establish two deanships: a dean of the college, provost, chancellor, vice-president for academic affairs, or whatever he may be titled, primarily the think man, administratively oriented but with a firm academic background, augmented by a dean of the faculty, who comes out of the faculty and whose major responsibility is translation of faculty feelings and roles to the dean of the college and president. The two of them work together and may very well both report to the president. This plan results in a division of labor in the deanship and hopefully reduces some of the tension of the middle man role which the dean historically has had. Departmental and division chairmen report directly to the dean of the faculty, while under the dean of the college are such activities as the library, the registrar, the admissions program (unless that is a student personnel activity), adult education, the computer center, institutional research, and, perhaps, institutional planning. Both deans make recommendations to the president on faculty and administrative appointments in the academic area. This concept produces not an assistantship but a codeanship enhancing the publics which the dean must honor.

The second proposed structure is essentially the same plan for the college presidency. Pattillo and Mackenzie suggest that an institution have a president who concerns himself with internal matters and a chancellor who works with the board of trustees and concerns himself primarily with external relationships of the institution.[11] Douglas Knight also suggested such a position upon his resignation as president of Duke University. Massachusetts Institute of Technology, Brandeis, Fordham, New York University, Fairleigh Dickinson, and Northwestern have adopted variations of this arrangement. Although this pattern does not directly affect the role of the dean in relating to the faculty, it does affect the total administrative impact on faculty relationships since one of the copresidents has considerably more time than previously to spend with the dean and the faculty and to assume the leadership role in academic matters, which could relieve the dean of much pressure.

In a third pattern, effective in a large or small college, the dean works entirely with the chairmen of the divisions of the faculty as his academic council. The organizational pattern can be one of appointment or election, one of advising or equal power. Either way the important features of this structure are that the division chairmen collectively assume full responsibility for faculty government, they relate their needs directly to the dean, and they share with him the responsibility of relating the faculty to each other.

This feature relieves the dean of the necessity of performing the task individually and independently. This pattern is simply a means of dispersing and sharing authority and power and exists at the discretion of the president and dean.

A fourth structure is an extension of the trio or cabinet form of college administration. In addition to the president, the development director, the business manager, and the dean, it includes faculty and student representatives who in turn report to the faculty senate and student government and serve as liaisons in interpreting administrative decisions made jointly by faculty, administration, and student representatives. The inclusion of faculty and students in decision-making bodies has expanded to include representatives of both groups on standing and advisory committees of the board of trustees, and in an increasing number of institutions faculty and students serve on the board itself, occasionally as voting members, sometimes as observers, and other times as unofficial nonvoting members. One hundred eighty-four institutions reported some such student representation to an Indiana University survey team, which indicated that students rarely reach trustee committee positions without the faculty's having gotten there first.[12] Two states have passed special legislation to enable faculty and students to serve on the primary policy boards of state colleges. Those trustees who are not willing to open full membership are increasingly establishing trustee-faculty and trustee-student liaison committees to increase direct communication and facilitate decision-making. That students and especially faculty contribute to administrative deliberations is certainly clear, but whether having faculty and students on trustee boards is a fad, a response in fear by trustees, or a genuine democratizing of education policy-making is not yet clear. In any event it is a very live organizational possibility for enhancing faculty-administration relationships.

A fifth way of organizing, attempted in some small colleges, is to return to the town meeting form of government with no separate faculty, administration, or student organization but rather a single all-college government with representatives elected equally from all segments. They constitute a college council or senate and make the major policy decisions of the institution. Although this form is possible in Pomona or Antioch, it is a very unlikely solution for larger institutions and thus has not gained great popularity. It probably is the most democratic form of government for an institution but at the same time may be so time consuming that faculty do not have time to teach, students do not have time to learn, and administrators do not have time to implement policy decisions.

No one of these suggested structures is a complete administrative organization effectively related to the faculty. All are partial efforts and could be combined totally or in units to move a particular institution toward a functional relationship which could, in turn, improve the teaching-learning process and product. Whatever the future organizational form of higher education in America, administrators will have to relinquish power, release more information, and renounce independent, free-wheeling decision-making processes for more democratic, slower, less efficient organizations which offer greater job satisfactions and, hopefully, better educational experiences for all.

References

[1] Four of these changes are cited and discussed at length in F. Rourke and G. Brooks, *The Managerial Revolution in Higher Education* (Baltimore: Johns Hopkins Press, 1966).

[2] *Ibid.,* p. 105.

[3] *Ibid.,* p. 111.

[4] J. Gould, *The Academic Deanship* (New York: Teachers College Press, 1964), p. 4.

[5] *Ibid.,* p. viii.

[6] *Ibid.,* p. 10.

[7] *Ibid.,* p. 40.

[8] *Ibid.,* p. vii.

[9] *Ibid.,* p. 5.

[10] *Ibid.,* p. 53.

[11] M. Pattillo, Jr. and D. Mackenzie, *Church Sponsored Higher Education in the United States* (Washington, D.C.: American Council on Education, 1966), p. 202.

[12] R. Muston, "Governance Changes Are Catching Colleges by Surprise," *College and University Business,* July 1969, p. 29.

4

Kingman Brewster, Jr.

Politics of Academia

The experiences of Yale—and other campuses—in the past few years have stimulated quite a bit of thought about how to make the work and direction of the university more responsive to the needs and interests of all its members. The main thrust of most of these reappraisals and proposals has been that there should be a broader and more democratic participation by students in the

This chapter is based on Mr. Brewster's speech to the Yale Political Union on September 24, 1969.

decisions of the faculty, and by both faculty and students in decisions traditionally reserved to the administration and trustees. The main issue has been not whether but how far this participation should be broadened, and how democratic the selection of participants should be. This certainly has been the focus of the discussion at Yale, both in the spring of 1969 by various student groups and unofficial "open" meetings and during the summer of 1969 in the deliberations of an ad hoc group of faculty and students who were asked to act as an advisory committee to Jorge Dominguez, a Yale College graduate of the class of 1967 and currently a junior fellow and candidate for the Ph.D. in government at Harvard University, whom I had asked to review the proposals and developments at other institutions and to recommend how Yale might best constitute a "legitimate" group of faculty, students, and others to make formal recommendations for the improvement of Yale's governance.

Champions of voting representation of students in all groups, committees, boards, and meetings make the appealing point that a student should be able to participate in the decisions which affect him. Now obviously his opinion should be taken into consideration, just as his interests should be taken into account. But the current mood is that he should be able to have a large say in making the final decisions on all matters. "Power-sharing" is the cry.

In past reports, speeches, and conversations I have encouraged the development of more avenues for student participation but I have also pecked skeptically at the notion of institutionalized representation as the cure-all for discontent, or as the principal prescription for improvement. Taking an advocate's aim at a straw man when he sees one, I have blasted the extreme and extremely silly notion that "pure" one-man-one-vote democracy would best determine the work and direction of a university. Although this opportunity was afforded by questions seriously put by an undergraduate editor, it is doubtful whether even he would have answered his own questions affirmatively.

Even if we could knock most radical participatory democrats and most reactionary traditional autocrats off their extreme perches, however, there does remain a fundamental choice of emphasis which must be made, yet which is receiving almost no attention. I am convinced that representation is not the clue to university improvement, indeed that if carried too far it could lead to disaster. I am, rather, convinced that accountability is what we should be striving for.

On some matters I have indicated before that the self-determination of the faculty, collective academic freedom from the pressure to please, requires that the faculty be able to meet in camera on issues of appointments, degree standards, and the recommendation of degrees. But leaving these sanctuaries aside, there is the very real question of whether it is in the best interest of the students themselves not only to make their voices heard but to try to govern the place. Put differently, it is pertinent to ask whether the place will be better or worse in terms of the student's own interest in the quality of his education if the responsibility for its direction is assumed by student representatives or if it resides primarily with the faculty and administration.

The answer to this question depends not only upon your assumptions about the relative wisdom of students in general and the wisdom of established faculty and administrative authorities, but also upon how truly representative you think student governors would be. I happen to think that in a world in which ideas and policies and institutions have a high rate of obsolescence, on many matters the young are more perceptive, wiser if you will, than their elders. On the other hand, experience has its claim. And in a self-perpetuating institution the claims of continuity have to be weighed against the claims of "now."

I am moved also by another very practical consideration, on the basis of admittedly short experience and inadequate sample. I do not think that the great majority of students want to spend very much of their time or energy in the guidance and governance of their university. They want to live and learn up to the hilt, and make the most of what they know to be a very unusual and remarkable short opportunity to develop their capacities by trial and error in the pursuit of personal enthusiasms. Over and over again this has been demonstrated even in times of crises which shook and threatened the existence of the institution. In the longer, duller life between crises it is even more demonstrable that to the average student the purpose of university life is learning and living, not governing. The long and unimpressive history of "sandbox" student government is fair warning that student politics, like the politics of professional associations, cannot be counted on always to draw out the most talented members of the constituency or to capture the attention and concern, day in and day out, of the eligible voters.

These misgivings have nothing to do with either skepticism of the motivation or scorn for the competence of those students who may be actively interested in university government. Their zeal is good for the university and a chance to participate is good for them. At best, however, they are a minority.

From time to time the opportunity for spokesmanship in the name of student opinion is seized by a wholly unrepresentative group. This may be by election, by the domination of open meetings, or simply by outlasting others who are less single-minded in their political interest.

So the first assumption which has led me to believe that broader sharing of responsibility for ultimate academic decisions is not the primary thrust of useful university reform is: The majority is not sufficiently interested in devoting their time and attention to the running of the university to make it likely that "participatory democracy" will be truly democratic. The second assumption is that most students would rather have the policies of the university directed by the faculty and administration than by their classmates. This is pure speculation; the question has never been thus bluntly put. The only reason I come to this conclusion, I suppose, is because I would feel that way. I would insist on a right to be not only heard, but listened to. But I think that the institution will do a better job and be more likely to make bold decisions swiftly and decisively if ultimate responsibility for its direction is sharply focused on the shoulders of people who are devoting their personal energies and risking their professional reputations for the quality of the institution.

Not only the capacity to make decisions boldly and consistently, but also the quality of those decisions urges that inherently executive matters not be distorted by being poured into a quasi-legislative process in the name of representation. If the allocation of resources is made a legislative process, it can only devolve into a pork barrel exercise with each interest group trying to take more and give less. The search for outside support cannot be dictated by any detailed legislated directive or control; needs must be matched to opportunities. The prospect of getting twice as much for the lesser need must be weighed against the chance of getting much less or nothing at all if other priorities are stubbornly insisted upon with all potential donors. As in all negotiation, individual conviction and intuition have to be relied upon. The delays and embarrassments of public discussion of particular approaches for outside support would chill the market and rob the executive of its ability to speak with the confidence and conviction which is the essence of selling the institution to potential supporters, public or private. Furthermore, there is an intangible element of character and personality on which any donor must rely when he puts his funds in trust. This would be diluted if the donor felt that the destiny of his gift depended on the rise and fall of political fortunes in a representative assembly whose members he could not possibly come to know with the intimacy which inspires confidence.

So, I am convinced that the political symbolism of participatory democracy is an illusion when applied to many of the academic and financial decisions which direct an academic institution and that the slogans of representative democracy could lead to even greater misrepresentation of the student interest in the quality of his institution if they implied the sharing of the faculty's academic responsibility. Either one, if carried to ultimate legislative supremacy, could stultify the capacity to steer the place boldly and decisively in times that require imagination and rapid change.

The answer to the legitimate student demand for individual self-determination is wider latitude for academic as well as personal choice, including the choice of whether and when to stay at the institution, now inhibited by an outrageous selective service system. The answer to the legitimate student demand to have protection against incompetent and unresponsive administration is not formal representation in all matters. It is administrative accountability. I would urge radical reform to make real the promise of administrative accountability precisely because I am skeptical of either participatory or representative democracy as a way of making final university decisions.

The first requirement of accountability is disclosure. Those affected by policies and decisions cannot hold those who make them to account unless there is full and adequate public access to the record of the process by which the decision was made. Good manners or simple humanity may make it from time to time desirable to impose a seal of confidence on one man's opinion about another, in the admissions or appointment processes in particular. Unless opinion can be received in confidence in such cases it may well either not be given or be watered down into banalities in order to avoid offense or injury.

There may also be situations where the intentions of the institution in its dealing with adversary outside interests make public disclosure very unwise. In an impending real estate deal there is no reason why the university should be deprived of its bargaining power by having to reveal its inner thoughts about an acceptable price. In a legal proceeding there is no reason why the university should forfeit its right to devise its strategy in confidential talks with counsel and others involved. But these are exceptions which can be reserved for executive sessions and confidential minutes. Hiatus could be noted in the record, specifying the nature of the problem and the reasons for exceptional confidentiality. Otherwise the record should be public. At the very least there should be a public communiqué. Literal transcripts would be even better. Even if such transcripts were rarely resorted to, their availability would be the best assurance that the university could not be governed by conspiracy and that the reasons given in explanation were in fact the reasons for decision. Obviously the self-consciousness which this would impose might be an inhibition; it certainly will be opposed by traditionalists who value the men's club atmosphere of confidential deliberation. However, some form of convincing access to the record of proceedings and the reason for decision seems to me far preferable to increased widening and diluting of the responsibility for decisions. If accountability as an alternative to representation is to be convincing, disclosure must be as nearly complete as possible.

The second requirement of accountability is the right of petition by those affected by decisions. There has to be a legitimate, easy, and reliable way in which critical opinion can be generated and communicated. Informal access through a variety of channels is the best way to do this in a relatively healthy situation. But if lack of confidence in authority spreads to a numerically significant minority of any of the constituent parts of the university—students or faculty or alumni for that matter—then there should be an understood channel of petition to whatever level is responsible for the appointment to the post or office whose conduct is the subject of complaint. If a large majority most of the time, or a significant minority all of the time, is willing to delegate the job of policy-making to faculty and administrative leadership, it is especially important that when this confidence is lost something can be done about it through legitimate channels. Accountability as a substitute for representation presupposes that those who are entrusted with responsibility will feel the hot breath of accountability day in and day out. This will be so only if petitions can reach and gain response from those in a position to act, at a level above those complained of.

The third essential element if accountability is to be real is some regular, understood process whereby reappraisal of the competence of administration and the community's confidence in it can be undertaken without waiting for a putsch or rebellion. At Yale this takes place regularly in the case of college masters, department chairmen, and deans. Every administrative appointment is for a term of years—three for chairmen, five for masters and deans. Naturally there is a presumption in favor of renewal if the man is willing. But after a second term there is an expectation that the man will revert to purely academic status as a teacher and scholar.

This expectation of impermanent administrative appointment has many obvious virtues. It passes the burdens of academic administration around so that over a generation more points of view are brought to bear, more people are involved and have seen the institution from the vantage point of important responsibility.

Hardening of the academic arteries is less likely to set in. Most important, the relatively short term assures both the institution and the man that there is an honorable and humane discharge which does not imply dissatisfaction on either side. Given this opportunity for periodic reappraisal, the president is in a position to solicit and react constructively to criticisms without waiting for the mobilization of malcontentment in the form of petition. Recent experience with the appointment of new masters and new deans has shown that a little time and trouble can bring to bear on such appointments the authentic views of the students and faculty affected. This should be no less true when the issue is renewal of an existing appointment, and any self-respecting, self-confident dean would welcome it.

But what about the president himself? For a couple of years now I have been toying with ways in which the president might be made more accountable to those whose lives and professional circumstance he crucially affects. While I do not think that his power can be fully shared by any legislative process, I do think that his own tenure should be at risk if he is to enjoy the latitude of executive decision which the job requires.

In thinking through the question of the president's responsibility in the case of a disruptive confrontation, I concluded that the power to act on the spot should not be stultified, but that in spite of all the dangers from Monday morning quarterbacks on the faculty, the president should submit his actions to review and should, if necessary, make the issue one of confidence. If he receives a vote of no confidence he should offer to resign. This attitude is implicit in my "Dear John" letter of April 1969, in which I tried to spell out our thinking about the protection of dissent and the prevention of disruption.

The principle of executive accountability as the price which must be paid for the exercise of executive discretion has, up to now, been formally limited to the power of the trustees to fire the man they hired as president. This is a terribly limited and inhibited power, since it cannot be exercised without running contrary to the expectation of a lifetime tenure. There is no objective occasion or event which invites the appraisal. Even the most decorous and covert effort to remove an unsatisfactory president is a matter of intense personal anguish to everyone concerned. Since it is likely to be resorted to only after deep rumblings of widespread dissatisfaction have been voiced in several quarters, the chances of concealing the reasons for premature retirement are very slight. If the malaise has erupted into rude, crude, and unattractive challenge, then of course the trustees are likely to get defensive, just to prove that they cannot be pushed around and that the institution will not be governed by mob rule. So the worse the disease, the harder the cure.

The essence of the problem is that while there is legal accountability to the trustees, there is no orderly way in which those most significantly affected by maladministration can invoke trustee action within a measurable time, without open challenge to the stability of the institution and the integrity of its processes. It seems to me that the only way this problem can be solved is to require the periodic, explicit renewal of a president's tenure. I happen to think that ten or twelve years is enough anyway, although there is no generalization valid for all times and places and people. More important than the length of average term, however, is the need for some shorter interval which permits periodic reassessment as a matter of course, without waiting for or requiring invidious or disruptive public complaint. Unless there is some such arrangement the hope for genuine accountability at all levels of authority is illusory.

I think Yale would be better off if it were understood that the trustees would make a systematic reappraisal and explicit consideration of the president's reappointment at some specified interval. This might be seven years after the initial appointment, perhaps at a somewhat shorter interval thereafter. I would urge the trustees right now to consider adoption of such a policy. Under present circumstances the effect would be to make the office more attractive not only for initial appointment but also for continuation in it. Of course the trustees could not, and should not, abdicate their ultimate responsibility for the exercise of their best judgment about the best interests of the institution. Occasions have arisen, and may well arise again, when defiance of student and faculty opinion is in fact justified by an issue of principle, just as may be the defiance of alumni or public opinion. Reservation of this duty and right, however, does not justify insulation of either the president or the trustees from a periodic, systematic assessment of what student and faculty opinion is.

Such accountability from top to bottom of the institution would require startlingly new measures for full disclosure of the meetings at which decisions were taken, and unorthodox revision of the terms of presidential appointment. Disturbing as such measures may seem from the perspective of inherited tradition, I am convinced that they would be far more consistent with the nature of a free academic community, and the administrative leadership it requires, than would the sharing of faculty and administrative responsibility for academic and institutional policies.

If such real accountability were achieved then I have no doubt that consultation would become regular, widespread, and serious. This should include formal as well as informal participation, including elected groups where appropriate. No one with any sense, let alone pride and ambition, could fail to take seriously the importance of adequate consultation with those to whom he would be held accountable at periodic intervals. Sometimes the processes of consultation will be best served by an elective process; sometimes it will best be done by trying deliberately to impanel a group with a greater variety of interests and viewpoints than would probably emerge from majority vote. Also there are mixed solutions, relying in part on ballot, in part on administrative selection. In any case, there should be no exclusive channel of communication or opinion, nor any requirement that all consultation should be formal.

"Legitimacy," if it were limited for the most part to consultative arrangements, might lose some of its rigidity. Even if ultimate responsibility should lie with the full-time faculty and administration, subject only to review by the trustees, consultative participation is not only good education for the participants but also a necessity if the institution is to be alert to its own needs in a fast changing society.

I make these somewhat radical proposals because while I do respect and share the dissatisfaction with a governance which seems free to ignore the will of the governed, I think that the sharing of faculty and administrative power with students on a widely dispersed democratic basis would be a disaster for our kind of academic institution. So I urge much more strenuous examination of techniques of accountability. They would be more fitting for university governance than would techniques for the sharing of ultimate responsibility with the transient student constituency. In order to further serious consideration of these possibilities I submit my proposals concerning disclosure and the terms of presidential appointment as worthy of consideration. Much more thought and inquiry is in order before such notions could harden into concrete proposals. They seem to me, however, to point in a direction far more promising than expecting actual direction of university affairs to come from a participatory democracy in which only a minority would participate, a representative democracy which would be unlikely to be truly representative, and the substitution of a legislative power for what are inherently executive responsibilities.

5

Robert S. Powell, Jr.

Student Power and Educational Goals

A lot of people in education today are doubting their sanity. Increasingly in the past years, enormous sums of money have been building vast universities; more students have been admitted and graduated than ever before. Our total store of knowledge has doubled since World War II. As a nation, we far outstrip the rest of the world in the degree to which we provide higher education for our people. Every available index seems to suggest unparalleled success for our higher education. Every index, that is, except the increasingly discordant feedback coming from the consumers—the students. They are marching, disrupting, sitting in, and generally making life difficult for universities and colleges from Berkeley to Manhattanville over some basic educational issues which have not been resolved to their satisfaction. I share this dissatisfaction.

Student power is fundamentally an educational principle, not a political one, and the focus in the first part of this chapter is on the basic educational aims of the student power movement. Yet, because the level of campus protests now threatens the operating futures of many of our universities, political questions are also quite relevant, and the second part of this chapter focuses on the more newsworthy problems of violence, civil liberties, and institutional survival—problems which the student movement has forced educators, public officials, and students to face.

We have strayed fundamentally in setting the goals of higher education. The goal of higher education should be to free people, by teaching them how to do their own learning. That means that higher education should move toward student-centered learning, a process whose primary purpose is to teach people how they learn best. This process should take place on an individual basis, and should involve the student constantly in the determination of his own program of study as well as in the policies of his institution. Learning must become a highly personal process in which the primary emphasis is no longer on the assimilation of a body of facts and knowledge, although that is often important for an individual who so chooses. If we can say that higher education has one single goal, it should be the encouragement of individual growth and self-development. Education should first and foremost lead you to know yourself.

The writings of psychologist Carl Rogers have had a profound effect on my own thinking about education. In *On Becoming a Person,* Rogers crystallized his view of the educational process:

> *It seems to me that anything that can be taught to another is relatively inconsequential, and has little or no significant*

influence on behavior. That sounds so ridiculous I can't help but question it at the same time that I present it. I realize increasingly that I am only interested in learning which significantly influences behavior. Quite possibly this is simply a personal idiosyncrasy. I have come to feel that the only learning which significantly influences such behavior is self-discovered, self-appropriated learning. Such self-discovered learning, truth that has been personally appropriated and assimilated in experience, cannot be directly communicated to another. As soon as an individual tries to communicate such experience directly, often with quite natural enthusiasm, it becomes teaching, and its results are inconsequential. It was with some relief recently to discover that Soren Kiekegaard, the Danish philosopher, had found this too, in his own experience, and stated it very clearly a century ago. It made it seem less absurd. As a result of the above, I found that I have lost interest in being a teacher.[1]

At the moment, however, our colleges and universities are operating from a much different perspective. Currently in higher education, the dominant goal appears to be not self-development, but rather job accreditation. Tests, grades, honors, degrees—these tangible signs of approval and success form the basis for what takes place in the classroom, and the students are taught that securing and achieving them indicate that one is "accredited" and ready to leave the campus to take a job reserved for those with such credentials. And, of course, the way one secures those credentials is to listen carefully in class to what the professors are saying, take rapid and complete notes, and, then, using the best memory techniques possible, return to the professor on the exam in a form as undigested as possible the facts and theories he lent the students during the term. If anything the man said during the term meant something to his students personally, or if his lectures helped in any way to sort out some of the important questions young people face today, all the better; but that is secondary to getting the course over with and on the transcript as completed satisfactorily. Robert Hutchins once observed that a college degree seems to certify that the student has passed an uneventful period without violating any laws, and that he has a fair, if temporary, recollection of what his teachers said; little pretense is made that many of the things said are of much importance.

In so organizing a student's college experience, an institution seldom has any hidden, pernicious motives in mind. To the contrary, the university views itself much like a consummate welfare state, deciding for the students the important questions of mind as well as body (required courses and required closing hours imply the same view of the student's capacities), but *always deciding for the student,* with his best interest in mind. This suggests that if we are serious about self-development as a primary goal of higher education, we must immediately confront the question of university governance. Currently, educational institutions are not especially democratic in their operations, and such an observation is consistent with their goal of job accreditation. Democratic process is not needed to decide whether the student has passed enough credit hours of lectures to receive the institutional stamp of approval and get the degree. If, on the other hand, we are aiming at the self-development of the students, and are trying to develop in them a capacity to take responsibility for their own learning, their own decisions, and their own work, then we must begin to move toward a more democratic university.

How would a more democratic university be different from the one we now know? First, we must move to abolish the current grading system. No step could be more central to basic reform. Grades are now the central instrument of coercion employed by the university against the students, and if students are to be allowed to participate and decide matters relating to their own academic plans, this instrument must be removed from the hands of the faculty. Grades are destructive of the very educational goal they purport to serve, namely, useful evaluation of learning. By testing the student's ability to memorize facts and notes, the professor discovers only the most superficial aspects of what the student has (or has not) received from a course. By giving the student a letter grade or a percentage score, he informs the student quite inadequately about the student's strengths, weaknesses, and future directions. Beyond this, however, the grading system sets the context and ground rules for student-faculty relations. The student performs, and the professor judges, and the relationship is strictly one way. Seldom is there any thought that the student and the teacher are somehow partners in the learning game; seldom any thought that perhaps the student might be competent to evaluate himself, for the record, and that such an experience in itself might be educative when done cooperatively with the professor.

In a sense, grades and required courses are campus monuments—monuments commemorating the failure of the faculty to persuade the students that they have something of worth and excitement to teach. Lacking this persuasiveness, unable to convince the students voluntarily that this or that course of study would be useful, personally rewarding, or intellectually challenging, the faculties of our universities have turned to the more coercive methods of education so frequently employed at the elementary and secondary level. By erecting an imposing array of requirements in the student's major, division, and degree field, and by substituting the grading system for the student's sagging motivation, the faculty attempts to ensure that no matter how bored or disgusted the student may become with what his teachers are offering, he will still perform.

Martin Duberman, who ran a series of experiments with ungraded classes at Princeton, recorded some interesting observations:

> [*Those who administer and teach in a university*] *make certain that the student's energies are directed at fulfilling tasks set by them rather than by the student. They encourage him to define his worth in terms of his success in winning their approval: high grades, good letters of recommendation, departmental honors, and so on. He is taught to regard these tangible signs of election as the only important evidence or kind of achievement, and as the indispensable precondition, almost the guarantee, of a satisfying life. What is not taught is that orientation toward gaining the approval of others carries high costs: the acceptance of disguise as a necessity of life; the unconscious determination to manipulate others in the way one has been manipulated; the conviction that productivity is more important than*

> *character, and success superior to satisfaction; the loss of curiosity, of a willingness to ask questions, of the capacity to take risks.*[2]

Let us be clear on one point: grades and useful evaluation are not necessarily the same things. Getting rid of the standard grading system will not be easy; we have been using it for so long that, like a narcotic, it has become an addiction, to the point that we are quite fearful of facing the world without grades. Often, we try to go halfway, by replacing grades with pass-fail, for example. While this alternative offers less coercion on the student to compete mindlessly for a better place on the normal curve, it still leaves the student without any substantive and useful evaluation of his work, which, after all, should be our goal.

A better direction would be to encourage the student and the professor to evaluate jointly the student's work and the professor's contribution to that work, with the evaluation being filed with other such evaluations in a personal dossier that the student builds during his stay at the university. The point is that a student ought to have a way of knowing what his skills and weaknesses are, but the grade point average is not the most sensible way, humanely or educationally, and new ways should be developed and tried at each campus.

There is a second step that should be taken if we are to build a more democratic university: the power of the faculty must be restrained. Currently the faculty exercises a virtual monopoly over the key academic decisions of the university—course offerings, degree requirements, programs of study, and all the other facets of educational policy. I oppose such power for two reasons. First, most faculties make educational decisions out of a particular and rather incomplete perspective. This "faculty elitism" is the attitude that what is taught in the classroom by a professor has an inherent worth, far beyond the effect it has on the students. Such a perspective tends to be visible in the curriculums that often come out of faculty deliberations—they appear designed to produce more faculty members rather than people with skills and capacities somewhat different from those possessed by professors. Second, few university professors know much at all about teaching and learning. Their competence within their subject discipline is not the issue; what is at issue is their competence to make educational decisions that embody basic concepts of learning and teaching effectiveness. The fact that there are so many bad teachers and boring classes on a given campus is partial testament to the point. One has only to read through the published course and teacher evaluations being put out by student governments around the country to get the clear impression that students are not terribly engaged by the majority of courses and professors with whom they come in contact.[3] Moreover, the hundreds of free universities and experimental colleges that have sprung up, student-initiated, around the country indicate that large numbers of students feel their learning experience can be organized in a much more effective and exciting way than the faculty has done it.

In a 1966 keynote speech to the American Council on Education, William Arrowsmith stated the problem:

> *I am suggesting what will doubtless seem paradox or treason—that there is no necessary link between scholarship and education, or between research and culture, and that in actual practice scholarship is no longer a significant educational force. Scholars, to be sure, are unprecedentedly powerful, but their power is professional and technocratic; as educators they have been eagerly disqualifying themselves for more than a century, and their disqualification is now nearly total. The scholar has disowned the student—that is, the student who is not a potential scholar—and the student has reasonably retaliated by abandoning the scholar.*[4]

One of the campus protest movement's substantial contributions in recent years has been its tendency to help all see more clearly the internal conflicts of interest that exist within the university, and especially the conflicts between students and faculty over educational policy issues. While students and faculty have frequently joined ranks to protest the Vietnam War, campus racism, or some other political issue related to events in the off-campus world, these two groups have become increasingly divided over internal disputes relating to the distribution of power within the institution. To a great many faculty members, student power demands involving shared power over curriculum, faculty hiring and promotions, and admissions to the institution appear to be nothing less than a bold and unwarranted intrusion of the incompetent (the students) into an area best left to the professionals (the faculty).

To be sure, faculties do have professional interests in maintaining a system that encourages research and authorship. Moreover, one should not be surprised that they resist the suggestion that their closed entry processes may be letting in the wrong people and rejecting a number of persons from whom the students would benefit. Such a suggestion not only attacks the process of faculty recruitment and tenure, it attacks the faculty as well. Yet, if such limited interests are, in fact, dominant within faculty bodies, it is not at all persuasive to argue that the interests of the students can be well served and faithfully represented by this group, which now makes all of the major academic decisions of the institution.

The interests of students in matters of academic policy are far too important to be left to the faculty. Those interests involve the quality of teaching, the excitement and utility of the various courses, the educational value of majors, departments, requirements, and degrees, the issue of admissions as it relates to students and faculty, plus many more. The recent history of the student protest movement suggests quite clearly that when push comes to shove on a campus over one or another of the above issues, the faculty will turn its back on the students and vote in the direction of its own self-interests. A frequent illustration of this point is the campus publish-or-perish controversy, involving a conflict over the retention of a good teacher who happens to be an infrequent or inadequate author. I have been personal witness to literally dozens of such cases, and the pattern is rather clear. After loud outcries from the student body, pickets, rallies, and all the rest, the faculty proceed to dismiss the offending professor with finality. One cannot help asking oneself, in the aftermath of such events, whose interests are being served here?

The monopoly now exercised by the faculty over academic policies must be broken. The way to break it is to make students equal partners in building the curriculum and in making all the related decisions about the university's academic affairs—grading, requirements, new courses, the academic calendar, admissions, degrees, and so on—including decisions about who gets hired and promoted on the faculty. The closed process we now employ for such decisions has produced an incentive system for professors that is vicious as well as destructive of undergraduate teaching and development. Few institutions reward a man for his teaching. Virtually all reward him for his research and publications, by hiring and promoting him if he does these things, and by holding him back if he does not. Only the student can add a third incentive to the mix—the incentive to be a good teacher, and to become skilled at helping people learn. If universities continue to exclude students from this area of policy, they shall continue to affirm that teaching and student development are not of the highest priority.

There are other steps to basic reform that will follow once students begin to participate in policy-making. For example, students should be encouraged to initiate their own courses for credit. Many universities now provide a simple mechanism for accrediting a student course proposal, a mechanism that operates quickly, in a supportive manner, and without endless committee red tape. Moreover, not only should students be free to plan, in collaboration with the faculty, their personal academic agenda; but they should be encouraged to do so. There is nothing sacred about the particular mix of courses now required for a degree, and, by encouraging the student to construct his own curriculum in consultation with professors, we might find that John Dewey was right when he wrote of the strong relationship in education between effort and involvement.

What I have written up to this point may make some sense to the reader; but does it speak to his basic and foremost concern about contemporary American higher education? The nature and depth of this concern on the part of many thoughtful people was revealed to me recently in a conversation with a very distinguished public official who has left government in search of new work. Not surprisingly, his excellent record as a progressive government official has attracted numerous job offers from universities in search of a new president. Yet, he has responded to these offers with considerable caution and hesitancy. He disclosed in our discussion a great deal of disquiet over what seems to him to be an endless string of violent campus confrontations between radical students and the university, confrontations which, to him, raised some rather sobering and serious questions about the future of the university as an institution of free inquiry and dispassionate learning. What kinds of universities will we have during the seventies, he wondered, if sizeable groups of students are prepared to prevent speakers from speaking on campus because the speakers may be pro-war or anti-Panther? What happens to a campus when it is frequently subjected to bombing threats, or repeated confrontations between radical students and the police, with all of the tear gas and bloodshed that go with such clashes? What does it say about the future of the institution when one of the topics discussed vehemently among a growing number of activist students is the wisdom of the First Amendment during times of a protracted radical struggle against the evils of American imperialism and racism?

Such concerns are, in my judgment, proper and well-founded. Many campus activists have abandoned nonviolence as a basic limiting principle of protest strategy. As nonviolence is abandoned, so are a number of the democratic constraints upon which our social relationships should be predicated—the reliance on persuasion rather than physical force to effect policy changes; the freedom of everyone to speak his mind, regardless of how distasteful his words or his presence may be to others; and the capacity of the majority of a community to determine community policies in a peaceful and democratic manner. These constraints are basic to a free society as well as to a free university. They are principles worth fighting for, a judgment widely shared on campuses even today. Yet, the tragedy is that those democratic constraints are frequently applied selectively by society's highest officials, and there is no finer example of this than on the university campus.

Certainly, the American university is one of the least democratic institutions in our society. Quite a few educators not only would agree with that assessment of the university, but would, in fact, applaud it. Yet, the consequences of such a pattern of organization are too frequently overlooked. Any institution which encompasses widely varying and often competing interests, in which the normal avenues of institutional change are closed to one of those interest groups, inevitably encourages the worst kind of undemocratic temperament among the disenfranchised. In the case of universities, the only power officials have in reality acknowledged the students to possess is physical power, the power to disrupt. Any student protest activity short of that has seldom produced policy changes demanded by the students.[5]

Persuasion and the rule of reason, which are so often heralded by beleaguered college presidents as the sensible alternatives to disruption, are principles around which students could unify, if they were operative. Sadly, however, official behavior in higher education indicates that a different set of government principles is being followed. As discussed earlier, grades, courses, credits, and the rest of what passes for higher learning is rigidly controlled by the "experts" on learning at the university, the faculty. The codes of discipline written by the institution to deal with improper student behavior are often so devoid of basic due process as to make civil liberties lawyers and federal judges shudder. The highly political decisions concerning the use of the institution's money in ventures tainted with war, racism, or some other social problem are seldom open to review by the students, but rather, are made behind closed doors by the trustees, who, it is said, are more competent in such matters. The decision as to who shall have access to the educational opportunities of the institution is likewise closed to student participation, even though that decision, like many of the others, is as political a decision as it is an educational one.

The list can be extended, but the point should be clear. The university's policies are not arrived at through any sort of reasonable democratic activity on the part of the students, and that fact cannot help standing in bold relief to the frequent pleas of college presidents to radical students to behave more democratically. Hence, even though many of the disruptive tactics of activist students are fundamentally contrary to our better notions of civil liberties, the university has left such students no reasonable alternative, and, consequently, the university must share the responsibility for their activity. During the academic year 1968–1969, when I served as president of the National Student Association, I had occasion to witness and often participate in student protest strategy sessions at dozens of institutions, including Wisconsin, Berkeley, Brandeis, Chapel Hill, Iowa, and Manhattanville. University officials, through their behavior during a crisis, repeatedly taught those student protesters this unfortunate lesson: that officials of the university could almost uniformly be counted on to behave evasively and with duplicity toward the protesters initially, yet would take the student demands with increased seriousness and responsiveness the longer the protest continued.

Only a fool could miss the basic political lesson to be learned here—namely, if you want to change university policy, do not waste your time with advisory committees and petitions; disrupt the place and *make* the officials deal with your demands. Moreover, one of the basic reasons such a strategy has been so repeatedly successful in winning concessions from the administration or faculty is that the consensus which governs most academic communities is so limited and fragile that even a small group within the community can shatter it with a demonstration. One can view only with sympathy and pity the terrible isolation of college presidents faced by a demanding protest group, when their pleas for support, guidance, and encouragement often fall on the deaf (or hostile) ears of the general student body and younger faculty. Yet, because students have had little or no hand in shaping institutional policies (either directly or through some representative system), one should not be surprised if their attitude toward the president's plight is either indifference or thinly disguised delight.

And the problem will get worse before it gets better. If it is accurate to characterize the difference in values and interests which separate my age group from that of my parents as a generation "gap," the millions of kids now entering high school will turn it into a chasm. This group is far more aware of the institutional constraints which inhibit free thinking and independent behavior in people than most of us were ten years ago, and they will have none of the treatment to which our universities now regularly subject students. Student power has become a high school phenomenon, and the implications of that for the future of our universities should not be lost on those who now feel total exasperation with the sporadic activities of a small handful of campus activists.

Colleges and universities can and should return to the peaceful task of helping people learn, but such a development will not take place, and in fact should not take place, in the absence of a fundamental alteration of campus governing procedures. I am specifically urging that students be accorded a measure of governing power in matters relating to all university policies, a measure equal to that now shared by the faculty and the trustees. Obviously, such a radical departure from current governing procedures cannot take place without a host of practical difficulties. No one should believe that creating a democratic university will be an easy or entirely satisfying task. Yet, for those who feel that such a step is essential, I offer the following practical guidelines for change.

First: Deciding upon the proper mechanism for student participation is a task that must fall to the individual campus. There are no universal solutions. The peculiar size, political history, and related local factors of each campus should be heavily weighted in deciding what mechanism to choose. For example, a campus community may decide that there are several different kinds of decisions made at the institution, each of which will require a different mechanism for student participation. Universitywide issues such as community relations, racial policies, investment issues that involve some political judgments, and the institution's relationship with the Department of Defense may all be properly adjudicated in an all-university council. On the other hand, decisions about course offerings, degree requirements, faculty hiring, tenure, and the like may best be decided within departments with the students in the respective departments participating equally with the faculty. Decisions involving the specific operations of an individual course may best be decided at an even lower level, between the instructor and the students enrolled in that course, so that a maximum of flexibility is preserved for both student and professor. Clearly what is required is a high degree of experimentation to find the right combination of mechanisms which preserves academic flexibility, yet ensures that the work and business of the institution get done.

Second: Reformers should expect no overnight miracles. Of all the groups that would be involved in these changes, the students are least ready to deal with them effectively. The considerable body of literature on experimental education at universities suggests rather strongly that students are initially confounded and uncertain when exposed to heavy doses of freedom and self-government. The Committee for a New Experimental College in Massachusetts (whose work resulted in the founding of Hampshire College) reported their struggle against student habits of dependence: "The most unmistakable result was an illustration of the extraordinary hold that the course system had on the minds of students and faculty, and the remarkable lack of sophistication of the normal college student when faced by an unstructured learning situation."[6] An even more revealing insight into this phenomenon was described by Goodwin Watson, who helped organize a program of experimental studies at Newark State College in New Jersey. He reported his impressions, in part, this way:

> *No characteristic has been more evident in most of the students at Newark State College than their docility. Many of them are products of strict parochial schools or of large regimented public high schools. They accept their assigned programs, arrive about on time at the designated classrooms, sit quietly taking notes while professors talk, buy the required texts, cover most of the assigned reading, and try to do well on the subject-matter tests. The first two years at college were rather like a continuation of their submissive high school years only in a different building. Some indeed were more active and involved and less passively dependent during certain high school courses than they customarily have been in college. The I.G.E.* [*Individualized General Education*] *program challenged this prevailing conformity and apathy. One of our first discoveries was that the students were bewildered and baffled by their freedom. They had no habits of self-direction and no guidelines of scholarship to guide them. They craved authoritative direction. It was several months before most of them rose to the opportunity to make their own curriculum in the light of their personal values, their intellectual curiosities, and their responsibilities as citizens of the contemporary world.*[7]

There is only one way for a student to learn the lessons of self-government and personal responsibility, and that is to practice those principles. A large number of institutions which have wisely abandoned their *in loco parentis* roles by turning over all questions of student discipline to student judicial boards have generally found that students have executed their responsibilities in this area quite seriously and effectively—much more so, in many cases, than the faculty had when it retained jurisdiction in such matters. The point is that such developments may not be achieved overnight, but may be preceded by an uncomfortable degree of temporary confusion and faltering, as the students attempt to cope with their new roles in the university community.

Third: Frequently, participation in university decisions may be as boring, tedious, and time-wasting to the students as it is now to the faculty. Not every important matter that requires a decision within a university embodies all of the apocalyptic politics of our times; in fact, the reverse may be true. Most decisions are relatively colorless and routine. Yet, such a characterization is not made in order to diminish the importance of such decisions from the students' standpoint. It is far easier to condemn the university's admission policies as racist than it is to set forth some practical guidelines for deciding who, among the thousands of applicants, shall be admitted, yet it is to that latter task that student representatives should be permitted to direct their energies.

Fourth: Students are as capable of being reasonable in their judgments about where the university should be going as is the faculty, but this does not mean that the two groups will always agree. While to some that proposition may seem patently obvious, it nevertheless needs emphasis in order to aid our understanding of what might happen if and when students are allowed to participate in university decisions. At a recent conference of academic deans I made essentially the same case for student participation that I make here. One of the deans responded by saying that his institution was now considering an enormous increase in the budget for the graduate programs, while keeping undergraduate development at about its current budgetary level. Would not the inclusion of undergraduate students on the committee faced with this decision, he wondered, all but sabotage his efforts to upgrade the graduate division? My response was simply to ask him whether he thought he could persuade the majority of the members of that committee, which included students, that his proposal was the best way to use the funds in question; if he could not effectively make that case to the committee, it would be my judgment that he should drop his proposal. Predictably, the dean was not satisfied with that response, for, in his judgment, decisions of that nature should not be open to such debate and argument. Rather, he felt that since the students might not be persuaded by his case, thereby preventing his proposal from receiving majority support, they should not be included on the committee. The illustration touches a fundamental issue about university governance. If we are to build a durable consensus on our campuses about what the university is and stands for in our society, we must acknowledge the right of all citizens of that "community" to participate in some significant way in the decisions of the institution. To organize decision-making in any other way is to make a farce of the word *consensus*.

Yet, to open decisions to students does not mean to completely reverse current practices on a campus. Students are no more and no less self-serving in their vision of what the university should be doing than are many of the other groups connected with the institution. Students are capable of developing a perspective which is sensitive to the many functions of the institution not immediately connected to undergraduate learning, including research and public service, but such a perspective cannot easily be developed in the absence of any significant opportunities to review institutional policies and alternatives with the faculty and trustees.

Fifth: Some may object to this entire notion of student participation on the grounds that it will mean less time for the students to spend on their studies. Certainly, one of the reasons young people go to college these days is to reap the benefits of reading a number of books, writing research papers, and engaging other people with their new ideas through seminars and informal discussions. It is also certain that student participation in university affairs will consume time that otherwise might be devoted to reading or writing papers. Yet, such observations overlook some important issues related to the meaning of a good education. First, an educational institution which actively discourages students from assuming a large measure of responsibility for the affairs of their own community is providing a disservice not only to the individual students, but to our society as well. It has occurred to me more than once that one of the greatest current social needs which can be uniquely met by our universities is for an increased number of citizens who are capable of thoughtful participation in public affairs. Universities should encourage that spirit among graduates by providing an experience in self-government for the students while they are on the campus. Moreover, whether it be at the individual course level or at the campuswide level, participation is learning, which is what the university is organized to foster, and that learning ought to be encouraged even if it means one less research paper each term.

Moreover, from the university's standpoint, student participation should be viewed as an essential element in institutional evaluation. If officials of the university are interested in the effect their policies are having on the consumers, that is, the students, they should be willing to include that group in their deliberations. If the students are not happy with the way things have been going, their voting behavior will reflect that dissatisfaction and will raise some important issues which otherwise may never be considered. Certainly that process will consume some amounts of student time, but that will be necessary if the university is at all serious about continuously reevaluating its performance.

Sixth: Some fear that student participation will result in arbitrary and indiscriminate reprisals against unpopular faculty members or unpopular ideas. To deal with that possibility, student participation should be coupled with a comprehensive university code which embodies the rights and freedoms of everyone on the campus, and the procedures through which those rights shall be sustained. At the top of the list of such rights should be guarantees of free speech and free press, substantive and procedural due process in any disciplinary action against a student or faculty member, and protection of students and faculty alike from sanctions imposed solely because of politics. Such guarantees are essential if the university is to return to the use of persuasion, as opposed to authority, disruption, or force, to resolve its internal conflicts. Such guarantees will not lower the level of conflict, to be sure; they will establish some basic rules for the game, however—rules which must be present if anything like a democratic system is to emerge from this new level of student participation.

Seventh: In arguing the case for a democratic university, I am not arguing for the kind of nonpolitical, socially detached institution which some would eagerly reconstruct. The university has been, and hopefully shall continue to be, a political—as well as an educational—institution, the affairs of which involve a great many ethical and moral questions. Those who argue that radical students have polluted the university's academic sanctity with their politics are not only factually incorrect, but naive as well. When millions of federal dollars have been poured into universities to help facilitate American counterinsurgency efforts around the globe; when admissions criteria have, with their definition of "excellence," made it almost impossible for black and brown students to gain admission to the campus; when ROTC has been accorded academic credit but draft resistance has been largely ignored or opposed by official university policy; when all these decisions plus a host of others are considered, it is not at all persuasive for the university to claim neutrality and detachment from social affairs.

Hence, when students make demands which relate to war, racism, or some other political issue, they are asking for a reordering of the university's politics, not an end to them. Not only would it be quite difficult for so large an institution to avoid politics, but it would also be irresponsible in a society so beset with problems as is ours. The point is that those kinds of decisions should be open to the entire community for deliberation and judgment, rather than left to a few trustees or senior faculty members.

The combination of reforms I have urged here underlines a basic principle: If there is to be reform within the existing institutional framework of our universities, it must be radical. Teaching and learning will not be restored to the campus by tinkering with the curriculum, by minor structural changes, or by modest innovations in graduate degree programs. These suggestions are offered not only because they are essential to the preservation of the university, but because I believe they are practical. Nonetheless, I offer them with considerable pessimism, in the doubt that there is presently enough energy and leadership in the American university for it to be reformed from within. The longer universities delay the task of confronting their own failures, and dealing honestly and vigorously with them, the more difficult the task of reform shall become. On this point, the comments of a thoughtful and perceptive college president, William Birenbaum, strike me as an appropriate conclusion to this analysis:

> *In my opinion, the tides of reaction against the young, the black, the poor, the powerless, the idealists, those searching for new commitments and for relevance are in full flow and have yet to crest. Those in charge, armed with their formidable powers to suspend, to redistribute the credit hours without consultation, to withhold the loan or scholarship, to regulate access to the lush middle-class job market, to influence the selective service status, to call police will successfully put down the students, the few radical young faculty, the SDS crowd, and the militant Afro-Americans. He who chooses reform will walk an increasingly lonely and dangerous road in the months ahead. He will be caught in a never-never land between the combatants in the law and order struggle that will continue to capture the headlines. Each side in that struggle will now retreat further from its own reality: the powerful, through brute force, from the reality of its own failure that caused the trouble in the first place, and the powerless, through more pot and even more outrageous disruptions, from the reality of a survival which depends upon getting an education they are not getting now.*[8]

References

[1] C. Rogers, *On Becoming a Person* (Boston: Houghton Mifflin, 1961), p. 276.

[2] M. Duberman, "An Experiment in Education," *Daedalus,* Winter 1968, p. 320.

[3] A good sampling of such evaluation can be obtained from the U.S.

National Student Association, 2115 S Street, N.W., Washington, D.C.

[4] W. Arrowsmith, "The Future of Teaching," reprinted in A. Eurich (Ed.), *Campus 1980* (New York: Dell, 1968), p. 118.

[5] This conclusion emerges repeatedly from the many high-level studies of college protest patterns. For a recent example see "Student Protest 1969," published by the Urban Research Corporation, 5464 South Shore Drive, Chicago, Illinois, 60615.

[6] G. Watson, "Individualized General Education" (Washington, D.C.: U.S. National Student Association, 1969), p. 7 (mimeo.).

[7] *Ibid.,* pp. 9–10.

[8] W. Birenbaum, "The American Campus: Whose Law and Order?" from a speech delivered March 5, 1969 (Washington, D.C.: U.S. National Student Association, 1969).

6

Robert Johnston

Student Culture and Student Power

The generation gap is not new. A struggle between the younger and older generations has existed throughout history. What is new about the struggle is that recently the younger generation has begun to win. Armed with moral fervor, lacking the inhibitions of their parents, more broadly educated than any generation in history, and communicating extensively and intensively with each other throughout the country, young people have increasingly demanded and won freedom from their parents and control over social decisions they think have been badly handled.

In a recent, rare appearance on Berkeley's Sproul Plaza, home of the original Free Speech Movement of 1964, Mario Savio made a statement clearly expressive of the consciousness gradually taking hold among today's students: "The future is ours as a matter of course." Faced with a barrage of media, mobility, education, and permissiveness among youth that can be neither comprehended nor rolled back, who can doubt a steady loss of power and authority over social decisions by the older generation? It is inevitable. No less inevitable, in the classic tradition of social liberation, is the accompanying massive unrest among the younger generation and the occasional ideological inconsistency and uncertainty. Active, aware students are growing spectacularly in number. Their ideas, their occasional militance, their resistance to once-adequate administrative sops, are spreading among campuses with the speed and power of a flood—unstoppable on a national scale, and to be resisted on individual campuses only through extensive authoritarian control. (Such controls have been forthcoming in a few instances, for example on a number of Southern black campuses, but would be unacceptable in most areas and if widely applied.)

The general thrust of student concern has been for lasting personal freedom and for a more egalitarian society to increase the availability of this freedom. War and poverty abroad, and poverty and oppression at home, are simply more than students will tolerate, and they are determined to root out whatever social values and institutions support these ugly social facts. There is a general determination to do this not in the manner of a new elite in search of power and authority, but in a reworking of the structures of power and authority themselves, to decentralize them and bring them closer to the people they affect. Today's students do not constitute a revolutionary vanguard, for there are too many of them. They are not intent on placing themselves in power while the slots and institutions they take over remain largely unchanged. They are more like a revolutionary tidal wave, numerous and pervasive enough to sweep out and take apart the whole house and rebuild it in a new image. In the long-run it is futile for the well-meaning administrator to ask them what they want, for most probably what they want is the abolition of his job. And this probability of course scares people. Institutions can totter, and it is probably a good bet that some will not survive.

On the other hand, the institution need not crumble. To abolish the job means doing away with the position and its power, but not necessarily discarding the man. If he is capable of working through the changes the students are trying to realize, and if he is capable of relinquishing large blocs of power to more open, humane, and rational processes of decision-making, then the institution itself will survive—changed but valuable. So the important question becomes, not what are the immediate answers to the contradictions latent in the means and ends of student ideologies, but what mechanisms can be established to arbitrate these contradictions and to make the results legitimate in order to maintain a functioning society?

I can hardly attempt a complete answer to this question, but can offer some tentative ideas. The mass media are going to be much less important and much less manipulable because new communication technologies are going to make the costs of entering this "marketplace of ideas" much cheaper. There is going to be a great deal of diversification of power out of the hands of the few men who wield it now. Likewise that second great bastion of mass stupefaction, the high schools, will be less able to pass on a received wisdom capable of pacifying large social groups, but will instead look at some of the more pressing needs of their students in terms of plain old reading, writing, and arithmetic. It seems safe to predict that students will have to be involved very heavily in the processes of social decision-making—this certainly is what they are insisting on now. It also seems safe to say that the procedures of this involvement will be decentralized but at the same time highly interdependent. Satisfying students will probably depend heavily on a very flexible curriculum, and on much more interaction among students within this curriculum than presently exists.

The insecurities and contradictions of uncertain values are certainly going to tax mightily the wisdom and finesse of faculty and administrators, as they already have, but a simple recognition of the concept that one goal of the community is to revise these values and social priorities in the interests of the society the students are fashioning for themselves, not to protect old decisions, will be to accomplish half the battle. If colleges could be built on the assumption that every generation has the right to fashion its own society anew, rather than to step into the worn-out shoes of its fathers, and if faculty and administration could recognize that they can facilitate the process but not direct it, then we could have at once an educational process very different, much more humane and much more effective than what we now have. Schools are presently organized and run, in large part, by nonstudents. This situation is going to have to change, first because the students are recognizing that they have the power to change it and would rather make the decisions which affect them, second because the students do not learn as much from an educational process in which they are not participating as from one in which they are.

It is often said that students in schools must be more cognizant of the hard *realities* with which they will have to cope on graduation. The fact they are more cognizant of them now than they have ever been surely is one of the reasons for the depth of their unrest. But at the same time the educational institutions, rather than giving them maximum freedom to experiment with alternatives to this reality under the sheltered umbrella of the university, do all they can to render the internal processes of change, innovation, consultation, and governance among students crass, impotent, and empty. Student governments are set up everywhere with neither power nor responsibility. Student newspapers are occasionally given power, or at least a degree of freedom, but then forced to conform to a version of responsibility dictated willy-nilly by nonstudents—which is more subtle but no less devastating than giving them no power. Everyone, of course, is quick to point out that the line has to be drawn somewhere. This is true, but it is important to understand, though it is almost never discussed, just where is a reasonable and effective place to draw this line.

It is clear that to the extent students are interested in developing alternative sets of social goals for their new society, they will want to use the protective and intellectually and creatively powerful umbrella of a community of learning. And they should be able to. Indeed there could be no better place (if there is any other place at all) where they can work on these questions in such a spirit of freedom. This is not to say that they should use this community itself as a bludgeon against an elderly society with which they disagree. Academic freedom must have some small price, but the price is that the implementation and execution of any kind or degree are matters the students must take up directly with the powers that be. Of course, the colleges have to be careful to ensure that they are not themselves among these powers; surely few can make a claim to such innocence just now. At the same time the universities must recognize that their first loyalty is to learning and scholarship, without which there is no very good reason for their existence, and that their second loyalty is to their students. With any different set of loyalties and values they court disaster through conflicting obligations and the pyramiding of social and political power into what might temporarily serve as beautiful edifices of government, but in the not-so-long run are internally corrosive and destructive of the freedom of learning and teaching upon which they are based. Social visions are going to come and go, even as generations and governments do; but if those universities which spawn them cling to them, they will ultimately go down with them, and processes of social renewal and improvement will be uprooted and destroyed at the source.

Knowledge, in other words, must be for all men.

This is why stratification in education has become so repellant. There is good reason for seeking out and lavishing attention on those motivated and capable of pursuing outstanding careers in scholarship. As I said above, the institution's first loyalty must be to this function. But there is no reason such emoluments ought to be specially available to anyone else, as the Ivies and other prestige undergraduate colleges now make them selectively available to the children of the well-to-do and well-placed. These prestige schools have been far more open in admissions in recent years, but their quality education is still available to a very small minority even though it could benefit many others fully as much as those privileged or lucky enough to be admitted.

Generally, I suspect that randomness in admissions processes would be far more fair and far more efficient than the arbitrary and self-perpetuating channeling that presently occurs. Everyone should have the same chance to go to Harvard or Yale, Michigan, or Berkeley, and once there the resources of the institution should be bent to see that everyone profits from them. We would at the same time learn much about student preferences and abilities and could set about to build the additional facilities that would fill their needs best, rather than build some gerrymandered version of population statistics and Scholastic Aptitude Test scores. Through their travels, their paperbacks, their records, and their underground papers students have developed an unprecedented potential for social mobility. Their schools could more profitably make use of this mobility rather than, as in old Southern relations between slave children and the children of the white master, cut students off from one another just when they are in danger of becoming really cohesive. There is simply too much invidious and discriminatory class separation remaining in this country, no matter how good our intentions, not to take advantage of every reasonable opportunity to surmount it.

Liberals have waited for the fringe militants to grow up and to acquire the stability and good manners and some of the moderated wisdom of age to stabilize their juniors, but this is happening painfully slowly at best. Neither the students, the radicals, the faculty, nor the authorities have been able to make much headway in creating expressive, fruitful channels of involvement for these masses of students, who seem themselves generally quiescent and undemanding of their environment.

As the graduate departments themselves are confronted increasingly with strong demands for shifts in emphasis in their research and teaching by the new young professionals, demands which are increasingly felt and eventually responded to, if only because these young men are the lifeblood of the central functions of the institution, one begins to see the whole huge system changing direction slowly and ponderously but, one hopes, surely. Just as surely, as these professional radicals rise in stature, their influence on the undergraduates will increase. The Berkeley campus will find itself caught more centrally in strains at least as great as any experiences to date in its relations with the general public which supports it, and in the internal processes of accommodation among various mixes of academicians, teachers, militants, and revolutionaries.

Media are like a social solvent. They are pervasive, powerful, and peculiar. Yet it is one of the great delights of students in the last few years that they have arrived at a *modus operandi* in relation to media which has been both ingenious and effective. On the one hand they have created alternatives in the undergrounds, in which they manage to reflect the cracks and aspirations of American society far more accurately than the straight press has, at least since the free-wheeling days of Horace Greeley. And on the other hand, almost as a stunt, they have learned to manipulate the newscasters, taste-makers, and self-appointed opinion-leaders, partly to expose their highly-touted omniscience, partly to put their own views before a public carefully protected from "subversive" ideas by a guardian press, and partly just to have fun. Unfortunately, although students have partially created this revolution in the media, they have not achieved similar change in the schools. But revolution in the schools is surely coming, and student demands are going to start reflecting it more and more. The number one influence will be by computers, and the number two by all kinds of exotic interaction with other electronic gadgets, such as TV, plus films. Today everyone says the computers are the most revolutionary invention since the book; but just as the church controlled carefully the laymen's use of books as long as possible, so the faculty is making sure that computers are kept in their hands, where they can make sure that to the extent the status quo is threatened, it changes in their favor. This state of affairs surely is not going to last very long. Students are going to demand access to their campus machines, and they are going to start experimenting with them in ways just as noisy, crazy and threatening as their other, off-campus excursions into news media. This experimentation may even spell the end, on the undergradute campuses, of the kind of restrictions on creativity ("but is it analytically, logically, or historically sound?" from a professor can pretty well nip most new ideas in the bud) that have dogged students to date. There will be an explosion of uses of TV, film-making, and computers, attended by a wide variety of distribution and application techniques among campuses nationally, and between campuses and the many communities and publics in the vicinity, now only loosely communicative with schools.

One of the most exciting aspects of students' demands on their schools has been their tendency to turn education on its head and, following Lewis Carroll, project it into the future. Alice thought it was "a poor sort of history that only worked backwards," and students are similarly beginning to realize that it is a poor sort of education that lays the dead hand of the past heavily across the future. Getting away from books will help avoid this emphasis on historicism. For students, equipped with computers, cameras, few inhibitions, and some good friends, education is becoming not so much a review of skills easily outdated, but a scanning and analysis of possible futures and possible means to reach them. Through interaction of their friends and machines, of their films, tapes, books, and periodicals, alternatives and ideas can be freely acted and tested out with the investment of a few hours, days, weeks, or maybe months, but hardly whole lives and careers. This generation's members can pursue many more roles, adopt in a lifetime many more careers and life-styles, and in a word enjoy many more futures, than anything imaginable just a few years ago. There has never been a time or place where a generation has not sought and fought mightily to take advantage of these kinds of opportunities.

Why resist?

It is true that most students are neglected and harassed in ways hardly consistent with democratic ideals or productive learning techniques, but it is also true that the less vocal the opposition among a study body, the greater the neglect and harassment is likely to be. Those 10 per cent of the student bodies doing 90 per cent of the complaining are getting 95 per cent of the benefits that are dished out to quiet things down. I have indicated that one reason the situation is true is because education in the great graduate institutions is generally so much better for the undergraduate there than elsewhere, and so much more selective in admissions, that talent, and the possibility for broad reform, are drained away. This is not to say that education in the great graduate institutions is better for undergraduates than at a few small prestige colleges. But these are very much the exception, and enroll a minutely small proportion of undergraduates in the United States—and the proportion is probably falling.

Society is on the verge of an egalitarian revolution in which there will be for the first time few poor as well as few rich, whereas now, as always in the past, there are millions of poor and hundreds of rich. Students are going to insist that schools reflect this change, that the pyramid narrow its base, push down its top, and expand the middle. It is an issue not of technology but of the distribution of resources. Prerogatives at the top are going to have to be shared a little more; and the possibility now exists for such sharing without destroying the cohesion needed at the top to hold the structure as a whole together. A well-educated society needs less central control to maintain its productivity. The relative redistribution of resources (that is, the channeling of growth resources not established ones) into this reshaping of the educational pyramid can foreshadow the most revolutionary social change and renovation, and the most extraordinary new society, we could dream of. That is where some students' heads are at on campus. Hopefully they will be able to take their campuses with them.

I have tried to make clear that considerable shifts of authority and influence in schools and considerable change in the processes of education will be needed to make these institutions truly responsive to the aspirations of their students and effective in their students' education for the very peculiar world we live in. Many students are interested in seeing bureaucracy, hierarchy, and curricular rigidity disappear. They want more egalitarianism and more freedom, and schools will have to be structured to adjust to these interests in more rational and thorough-going ways than they are now. Higher education in the United States is predominantly organized around standards and procedures set in a very few elite institutions. The elite are wont, whatever else they may do and however well, to protect their elite status. This relegates anyone not privileged enough to attend one of these best schools to a second-class status. Of course we are told these fine few have their standards to uphold; and maybe they do at the graduate level. But these standards are irrelevant and unnecessary for more general purposes, they are in fact discriminatory, as we are learning from the blacks.

It is time for a degree of twentieth century specialization of function. Many have said that the historic functions of universities have been the preservation of knowledge, the transmission of knowledge, and the production of new knowledge. It is easy enough to understand the close link between the first and the third, since research and scholarship are so closely intertwined. But as the need for new knowledge mushrooms on the one hand and the number of students to be educated in the rudiments of knowledge mushrooms on the other, one would suppose that a broader review of these functions might be in order. There are probably not more than twenty-five universities in this country that play a significant and irreplaceable role in these functions of research and scholarship, the rest being in this respect simply second-rate window dressing, even as they spend great amounts of money trying to emulate the masters. This is a sham and a waste of resources. On the other hand, these twenty-five great universities are irreplaceable and priceless, perhaps the single greatest resource this society possesses, and unique in history for their breadth, size, number, and diversity. Their importance should be recognized and they should be supported accordingly. At the same time it should be clear that their human resources are limited, and their functions ought to be similarly restricted. In a word, with the undergraduate population burgeoning, it is unreasonable to most students and to these centers of knowledge to make them undertake huge programs in general education. Further, there are very heavy and important demands on schools to attend more closely to a fourth function, social service. Surrounded as we are by social ills, and by students who feel very strongly the need to set to work on them, this function might well be considered a central purpose of general education. But here again, it is a great burden on institutions as they are presently organized to make an effective contribution to such service. There is no immediate necessary correspondence between great scholarship and social service. And to confuse these functions is to dilute and misdirect their application.

These great graduate institutions ought to be set apart, where they can continue to pursue their great work in a comtemplative atmosphere appropriate to their tasks. They need be no more isolated in this work than they wish, but at least they can decide for themselves how best to function rather than be subjected to a barrage of conflicting and pressing demands from governments, publics, and undergraduates. This done, the national freedom and egalitarianism that students feel is so important to them can be nationally provided for. Once the educational institutions are free to undertake in earnest the enormous educational tasks society is putting on them, we might hope for many times the attention to that task than is now the case.

If Berkeley, Harvard, and Michigan have succeeded to date, under various kinds of considerable pressures, in providing an education for undergraduates worth having, they have done so at the cost of perpetuating educational structures and attitudes which have had no end of ill effects on the great and growing masses of undergraduates not so privileged as to be able to attend these institutions. If these schools' great faculties can still maintain an undergraduate program with hardly a trace of student participation, autonomy, or flexibility, well and good. But they are most certainly rare in this respect—there are few such brilliant faculties. If these schools can be administered in day-to-day affairs with hardly a trace of student influence, except from the streets, and still keep students involved and active in their education, with good to excellent results when they graduate, then again they are surely the exceptions among most colleges and universities in this respect. So, while it may be true to say that a student at Harvard or Berkeley, Yale or Michigan, is getting a better education than ever before, and still the best in the world, the question is, what about everyone else? Do they not deserve a crack at something besides second and third-best?

I think they do, and I think that the only way this can happen is to let these brilliant faculties do what they are best at and want to do anyway, graduate training tied to scholarship and research, while the rest of us get back to education. Administrations, publics, funders, cadres of teachers, and the rest cannot serve two such diverse gods and serve them well when there are so many conflicting pressures. Everyone involved may be completely altruistic, but inevitably decisions are made and priorities set which will shortchange somebody, and it should be clear that it is currently students who are most vulnerable because now they are inevitably at the bottom of the table. Even now, as student unrest mushrooms, we see an atmosphere of "promise them anything, but give them a committee." The real changes are microscopic. The schools should be a constantly changing panorama of new publications, news media, new courses, new teachers, new field work, new projects, and new futures of all kinds.

Students have to learn to develop a diversity of skills of a broad range—personal, interpersonal, intellectual, man-machine, and more, few of which are even remotely encouraged or supported on campuses now. They must learn to think and act freely, yet cooperatively. They must learn that privilege and authority are outmoded in this post-capitalist society, and that meaningful values can be as shared as they are diverse and unique. Yet fundamentally they will learn none of these things, and their new societies will suffer from their absence, until their schools do. The sooner the better.

University administrators troubled by students' complaints that they are failing to provide an undergraduate education suited to the complexities and difficulties of our times, not to mention effective in getting students to learn, may ask themselves the following questions.

How many new courses were there on your campus this past year? If knowledge is increasing over 10 per cent a year, you could try for at least half that percentage rate of new courses for undergraduates.

What was your ratio of expenditures in libraries, computers, films, TV, and other gadgets, *for students,* to your faculty salaries budget? Five per cent would be a very modest starting figure, 10 per cent a minimum figure to really make a difference, and growth should be twice as fast as the faculty salaries budget to keep up with this changing world.

What is the average age of your administrative staff, not

counting clerks unless they are directly involved in helping you make or administer decisions (which is something you might consider)? If it is over forty, you are going to be neither very fleet-footed in dealing with public and student demands nor very in-touch with the substance of changes pressing in from all sides.

How many deans, department chairmen, and administrators of all kinds have at least one student among the circle of committees and informal contacts regularly consulted about current issues? Until it is 90 per cent you have no cause to sit back and relax and be proud of yourself, and until students fill at least a third of those consultation slots, you can assume you have still got a ways to go toward involving them in their own education.

When was the last time you told your trustees, state legislature, or whatever erstwhile power-that-be that they were at best out of touch and misguided and at worst elitist, and that they ought to listen more, talk less, and think a little less of themselves for it? If not within the past six months, there is probably a communications gap somewhere, and it is going to come back and haunt you sometime soon.

7

T. R. McConnell

Faculty Government

Profound changes in patterns of authority and influence are occurring throughout higher education. In some institutions there is an internal struggle for participation and power among students, faculty, administration, and trustees. In response to campus disruption, external forces are increasing their pressure on colleges and universities. Legislatures are considering punitive laws for controlling disruption and violence. Some governors are asserting political or personal power over public institutions. Pressure groups—from the left to the right, from the influential elites to the dispossessed minorities—are trying to use universities to protect their interests or to realize their aspirations. Systems of public institutions also are impinging on the autonomy of member colleges and universities, in many cases leaving institutions frustrated in determining their own destinies.

Changes in influence and control have occurred over a long period. Recent changes in federal support for higher education and in student rebelliousness have greatly accelerated the redistribution of power. The transformation has only begun. McGeorge Bundy observed recently that "the distribution of authority and responsibility among the various members of the university is now in question as it has not been for generations."[1]

One of the most significant changes since World War II is the great growth of faculty power, coupled with rapid faculty professionalization. Either by formal delegation or by tacit approval, college and university faculties have attained a high degree of professional self-government. They control education for and entrance to their profession, selection, retention, and promotion of their members, the curriculum, work schedules, and evaluation of their own performance. The individual faculty member's independence is enhanced by the principles of academic freedom and tenure. With increasing professionalization, he has attained a substantial degree of personal autonomy. Consequently, says Bundy, "when it comes to a crunch, in a first-class university it is the faculty which decides."[2] In the future, faculty authority may be eroded by forces both inside and outside the university; but at present faculty power is significant enough to deserve close analysis of the means by which it is exercised and the larger role it should play in the governance of colleges and universities.

Increasing faculty professionalization has tended to curb the authority of governing boards and administrative officers. Some years ago, the president of a large Midwestern land-grant university was reorganizing the institution by fiat with little or no faculty consultation. Having established its athletic prowess, the university had begun to recruit able scholars to its faculty. I remember remarking to one of the vice-presidents that if the administration wished to complete the reorganization of the university by directive, it should do so quickly because a much more distinguished faculty would not permit it to act arbitrarily.

Size and increasing professionalization have left only vestiges of collegiality in faculty government. Some years ago, standing in the court of one of the quadrangles, a member of Oxford's St. John's College, which then had only about 200 students, observed that in that small enclosure the Fellows often met informally to decide many of the questions facing the college. This is the picture of a true collegium. In most of our large institutions there are few evidences of an academic community; perhaps collegiality survives in the departments. But departments—in the larger institutions—themselves embrace so many different specialists who are unable to communicate with one another that here, too, little community remains. Perhaps the collegium survives in cluster colleges. Community life may have been restored in small experimental colleges in large institutions, but the larger environment of the multiversity is often a constant threat to close collegial relationships.

As institutions have grown in size and complexity, they have organized hierarchically. Even the faculty has had to structure itself bureaucratically in order to carry on its business. The teaching staff creates representative senates to act for it, and establishes an elaborate system of committees. "In short, the so-called academic community becomes less of a community—an informal collegium—and more of a formal organization, in the faculty itself as well as in the administrative group."[3]

Except in crises, a limited group of faculty members conducts business for their colleagues. The report of the Study Commission on University Governance at Berkeley observed that "there is a marked tendency for a relatively small number of faculty members to monopolize the membership of the most powerful committees and to rotate the chairmanships among themselves."[4] In other words, oligarchies take over the machinery of faculty government. The Study Commission observed that the combination of Academic Senate oligarchy and bureaucracy tends to discourage appointment of faculty members with unorthodox or dissenting views to major committees. The oligarchy tends to be essentially conservative.

Under ordinary conditions, ruling elites take over faculty affairs. This has recently been documented in a study of senate committee membership for the period 1965–1968 at the University of Minnesota. The study revealed that during these three years 10 per cent of the university staff had served as members of three to six different senate committees. Furthermore, a little more than an eighth of the committee members had accumulated six to ten years of committee service. Thus, a small number of people were potentially able to exert a high degree of influence on faculty and university affairs. The Minnesota committeemen were also elders, at least in rank. Approximately 85 per cent of them were from the two senior ranks, and more than three-fifths were full professors. The scanty representation of faculty at lower ranks and ages gives a relatively conservative cast to the formal faculty power structure.[5]

A comparable record of participation in faculty government was found at Fresno State College in California. Over the three-year period 1965–1968, 44 per cent of the faculty eligible for appointment served as members of selected major senate committees. Fifty-six persons out of a faculty roster of 417 served on three or more different committees during the three-year period. Sixteen of these served on four committees, and seven on five. Full professors composed from 53 to 83 per cent of each committee. Faculty members at lower ranks served mainly on the Student Affairs Committee and on the Budget Committee, which was relatively inactive. Again, one finds the same concentration of participation and, presumably, concentration of power in faculty affairs.[6]

A study of senate committee service at Berkeley for the ten-year period 1957–1967 showed that two-thirds of a representative faculty sample had served on no senate committee. Of those who had served, forty-seven, or a little more than 10 per cent, had been members of three or more committees. Among committee chairmen the concentration was greater: of 138 chairmen, fifty, or 36 per cent, had served on three or more committees. From 54 to 61 per cent of committee members were full professors, and from 67 to 76 per cent of committee chairmen were at the top rank. The Budget Committee, one of the most powerful at Berkeley, not only in budgetary policy but also in faculty appointments and promotions, was composed solely of full professors. Only four of fifty-two members of the important Committee on Committees were below that rank. Committees on which other ranks had served with considerable frequency included those on elections, prizes, schedule, student affairs, and undergraduate scholarships, which have relatively little to do with faculty power.[7]

Essentially the same pattern of participation in faculty government characterizes all three institutions. The degree of participation in senate committees is relatively limited. A very small number of faculty, while not completely monopolizing membership, engage extensively in committee service. The most powerful committees are heavily weighted with people at the top ranks. The oligarchs constitute what is essentially "the rule of the elders." With these academics in power, one would hardly expect galloping educational reform.

The emergence of oligarchies or ruling elites is normal in democratic polities. Political analysts have divided the voting population into gladiators, spectators, and apathetics. Gladiators, a relatively small corps of "professionals" constituting something like a tenth of the population, are the political activists. Under normal conditions, the rest of the electorate permits the oligarchs to rule with relatively little interference. This small group governs without consultation except with the particular minorities or clienteles directly affected by their decisions. When crises arise, however, the larger group of spectators enters the political arena. Presumably, once the issues are resolved, the spectators can return to their previous role as potential activists. The possibility of their engagement serves as an important restraint on the oligarchs' freedom of action. The apathetics, roughly a third of the electorate, seldom participate in political activities and usually do not even vote. They enter the political arena only under extraordinary and provocative conditions.

The same categories apply to the academic community. Since the faculty senate or the faculty as a whole, especially in large and complex institutions, lacks the capacity to make decisions expeditiously and to act accordingly, the gladiators or oligarchs carry on the day-to-day business. When campuses are relatively quiet, they do so without being challenged very often or very contentiously. When a campus erupts, on the other hand, the potential activists move in, and some of the apathetic constituents may also be aroused. Dissident minorities, sometimes aided by such "political parties" as the liberal Faculty Alliance at Berkeley, which stemmed from Free Speech Movement days, may try to carry the vote in senate meetings or to reconstitute the ruling group to include some of their own members. Frequently, probably usually, this effort to change the power structure fails. After the Free Speech Movement at Berkeley, some of the faces of the oligarchy changed, but the Establishment survived without making many concessions.

Oligarchies are frequently casual about their accountability to the general body politic, although they may be careful to consult the particular clienteles who are especially interested in certain decisions. At Berkeley, before the series of crises which began with the FSM, the reports of even the most powerful senate committees to the senate itself were perfunctory in the extreme. After the disruptions, which provoked much more widespread temporary faculty participation in senate affairs, the committees began to make much more substantive reports.[8] Whether this more active accountability would survive a return to a peaceful campus—an unlikely contingency in the near future—is doubtful.

Under normal circumstances, oligarchs establish special relationships with the administration. The Berkeley Governance Commission quoted the report of a subcommittee of the Senate Policy Committee to the effect that "the committees have become so intimately involved with administrative officers in policy formulation as to be virtually incorporated into the administrative machinery; and in fact many senate committee members have moved easily and naturally into regular administrative positions."[9] Actually, the oligarchs maintain a shifting balance between their faculty clienteles and the administration. They move in one direction or another, depending on the issues and on the pressures and faculty interest groups involved. If the ruling group associates itself too closely with the administration, it tends to lose the confidence of its faculty constituency. On the other hand, if it identifies too exclusively with faculty interests and values, it may lose the confidence of its administrative confreres.

The formal relationships between faculty and administrative lines of authority vary from institution to institution, and one cannot always infer the nature of such informal relationships as those mentioned in the preceding paragraph from the organizational structure. At the University of Minnesota, administrative officers serve on many senate committees. A recent study showed that, excluding student and alumni members, nearly 10 per cent of the total number of committee appointees were members of the central university administration, and another 41 per cent were deans, associate or assistant deans, or directors of special programs. When department chairmen were included among administrative officers, two-thirds of all appointments of staff members to senate committees were persons with some administrative responsibility. This same proportion had obtained in comparable studies made one and two decades previously.[10]

Likewise, at Fresno State College the president and the academic and executive vice-presidents are ex officio members of the senate. Although there are no members of the central administrative staff on four senate committees, such as the Committee on Committees, central administrative officers are ex officio members of all major collegewide committees.[11]

Quite a different situation exists at Berkeley. There, the elected Committee on Committees almost never appoints a central administrative officer to senate committees. Joint membership of faculty members and administrators presumably makes it possible for administrative officers to participate in decision-making throughout the process. If they have no access to the structure of faculty government, they have to act on committee recommendations without prior opportunity to introduce relevant information, to make proposals, to suggest alternative courses of action, to sketch the broader context in which particular decisions should be made, or to negotiate differences. In other words, the exclusion of principal university officers from membership on senate committees almost precludes effective administrative leadership. Furthermore, exclusion sets the stage for confrontation; that is, committees face a responsible administrative officer with ready-made decisions which he must either accept, attempt at this late stage to have the committee reconsider, or veto. The Berkeley Governance Commission declared that the chancellor himself should remain aloof from senate debates and committee deliberations. This separation, said the commission, "would achieve two objectives: it would encourage forthright debate, yet it would protect the 'distance' and comprehensive perspective which we regard as the essence of the chancellor's leadership."[12]

One of the consequences of the omission of central administrative officers from senate committees at Berkeley is the long roster of administrative committees appointed by the chancellor, sometimes with suggestions from the senate Committee on Committees. One finds, then, two parallel bureaucracies—the faculty committee structure and the administrative committee organization. There is often little collaboration and usually little liaison between corresponding committees of the two jurisdictions. This dual structure would seem to set the stage for cumbersome decision-making, inconsistent recommendations, and possible conflict between senate gladiators and central administrative officers. Under stress there is considerable tension between faculty and administration at Berkeley. It is extraordinarily difficult for faculty and administration to combine efforts in educational development or reform. Finally, it is difficult for administrative officers to exert educational leadership except through such informal devices as the chancellor's Academic Council, an essentially "extralegal" body composed of deans and chairmen of major senate committees.

In contrast, at the University of Minnesota there have been few instances over the last decade of serious differences or great tension between faculty and administration. It seems reasonable to assume that the close collaboration of administrative officers and faculty members in major committees is one reason for the relatively high degree of trust that characterizes faculty-administrative relationships at Minnesota.

It would be unwise to assume that the distrust at Berkeley and the rapport at Minnesota are the products of administrative inclusion or exclusion on senate committees. At Fresno State College, as pointed out above, central administrative officers are ex officio members of all collegewide committees except those which are designated explicitly as senate committees. Thus, the Fresno administrators have the opportunity to participate fully in the decision-making process. Yet a large segment of the faculty, although not the majority, suspects the motives of central administrative officers, resists their participation in decision-making, and seems to desire confrontation more than collaboration. It is obvious that factors other than joint participation are at work. They include such matters as the behavior of governing boards, administrative style, faculty unionism and struggles for power among faculty factions, the degree of decentralization of decision-making authority (faculty and administration may tacitly agree to divide responsibility and authority and to keep out of each other's way), political intervention, and constraints of system membership and coordination.

We can anticipate, at least in the near future, in most institutions of higher education a tendency toward greater conflict between the administration and the faculty. After recounting the changes which have accentuated the segregation of administrators from the rest of university life, Lunsford observes that "a major effect of these changes has been to erode the informal relationships between administrators and faculty members, relationships which engendered and sustained the trust necessary for an easy exercise of administrative authority, and which muted the potential conflict between administrators and academics in the university of an earlier day."[13] His analysis of the ways in which administrative officers have attempted to bridge their separation from faculty members and from academic affairs implies that there is an irreconcilable difference in the values of scholars and administrators that makes tension, controversy, and even conflict almost inevitable.

Gross and Grambsch have reached an opposite view of faculty-administrative relationships. They asked both faculty members and administrators to indicate on a five-point scale how much emphasis they felt certain goals actually received at their institutions, and how much emphasis the goals should be given. Their analyses "give no support to the contention that administrators differ so much in outlook from faculty members that the goals they emphasize, when they have power, run counter to faculty interests." They found so much correspondence between the values of faculty members and administrators, and so little discrepancy between perceived and preferred goals on the part of either group, that "whatever discrepancies exist between what is and what ought to be are not serious or pervasive enough to create tension that would cause the faculty member or administrator to leave." Where tension did exist, it was between faculty members and outside agencies: "With respect to the relation between power structure and goal emphases, the dichotomy is not between administrators and faculty members: it is between the 'outsiders' (legislators, the state government, regents—who though technically within the university actually share little in its day-to-day life) and the academicians."[14]

How may the apparent discrepancy between the views of these investigators be explained? Lunsford suggests that the administrator tries to diminish his alienation by building a set of myths to span the gulf between him and the faculty. The administrator believes that he attains rationality by consulting faculty members, and now, possibly, students. He identifies himself with the institution and imputes to it the goals and values which, he hopes, will unite the members of the academic community. He assures himself and others that he is entirely nonpolitical in making decisions. If his actions do not coincide with the faculty's recommendations, he asserts that they reflect the broader interests and functions of the institution.

If Lunsford is correct, one suspects that the administrators in the Gross and Grambsch study, acting consciously or unconsciously on the myths by which they have tried to explain their conduct to themselves and to the faculty, professed that their values and goals were the same as those of the academics. I suspect that the real discrepancy is much greater than the questionnaires revealed. I am inclined to the view that tension is inherent in relationships between faculty and administration.

Various means of reducing tension or conflict have been adopted or proposed. One of the devices which characterizes the multiversity is its decentralizing of decision-making authority to the lowest possible levels of the organization, and holding central review by either faculty bodies or administrative officers to the minimum. Thus, at the University of Minnesota, personnel decisions and curricular actions are taken at the departmental level, although they may be at least perfunctorily reviewed centrally in some of the schools and colleges. However, there is little intervention in these matters either by universitywide faculty bodies or administrators. If tension reduction is the principal goal to be attained, decentralization of authority is apparently a useful device. Whether it is productive of either educational integrity or budgetary efficiency is quite another matter.

With the advent of student disruption and rebellion, proposals have been made to divide authority formally among the elements of the organization as a means of avoiding or minimizing conflict. For example, in establishing the Berkeley Commission on University Governance, the Academic Senate directed the commission to determine "those areas in which, and the institutions through which, the making and administering of policies should be delegated wholly to students or wholly to faculty or administrative officers; those in which students should have primary responsibility, with participation by faculty members and administrative officers; and those in which faculty and administrative officers should have primary responsibility, with appropriate participation by students."[15]

If the commission had followed this charge, it would presumably have recommended a combination of segmental autonomy and shared authority in the university. In its report, however, the commission rejected the separatist model in favor of an arrangement premised on the values of community interaction and responsibility that would be continually shared. The commission held to this position even in the case of student participation. It concluded that few student interests could be successfully acted on by a student organization that is separate from the general process of campus decision-making. The task of the commission was to overcome segregation by incorporating students into the decision-making process through various institutional means, rather than confining them to haggling over the peripheral powers of the separate student organization. However, the incorporation of students in decision-making has turned out to be a vain hope. The Berkeley Academic Senate has consistently declined to include students in the membership of its major committees.

In the meantime, the University of Minnesota has turned to a modified bicameral system of internal governance. An Academic Senate task force first proposed that a relatively large number of student representatives be added to the senate. The senate failed to approve this proposal, and instead, toward the end of the academic year 1968–1969, established a tripartite organization composed of a Student Senate, a Faculty Senate, and a University Senate, with a general distribution of functions among the three bodies. It remains to be seen to what extent final power will be delegated to the Student and Faculty Senates, and what matters will be the subject of joint action. A contest over power and jurisdiction may well take place.

Closely related to the struggle for power in college and university governance are the methods used for resolving controversy and conflict. The issues are exemplified in the attitudes which distinguish the American Association of University Professors (AAUP) from the American Federation of Teachers (AFT). Crudely put, the division is between the principle of shared decision-making and shared authority in a community with common interests, as espoused by the AAUP; and the assumption of permanent conflict of interest between faculty and administration requiring confrontation, collective bargaining, and coercive sanctions, as held by the AFT.

The AAUP's principle of shared authority and responsibility has been defined as follows: "Among the faculty, the administration, and the governing board there is an inescapable interdependence and . . . these three components have joint authority and responsibility for governing the institution. . . . The essential and overriding idea is that the enterprise is joint and that there must be 'adequate communication among these components, and full opportunity for appropriate joint planning and effort.' "[16] The policy of the AFT, on the other hand, is to confront power with power. Using the industrial analogy, Israel Kugler, president of the United Federation of College Teachers, AFL–CIO, put the position as follows:

> *The board of directors is the board of trustees; the managers are the presidents and the host of deans. It is these groups that wield the power and authority and determine the destiny of a university. To be sure, they have woven a web of faculty senates and councils which simulate the original role of policy-making that university faculties once had. The advisory nature of these bodies provides them with some active role in curriculum and student affairs, but virtually no part to play in securing the necessary finances to provide professional salaries, work load, and working conditions.*[17]

The effectiveness of shared authority depends on rational means of resolving controversies, agreeing on purposes, and criticizing and affirming values. "Appeals to common commitment by reason and persuasion, the pressure of opinion, the judgment of colleagues," said Kadish, "—these are the informal sanctions which cement the academic community and which administrators and governing boards, no less than professors, have a professional obligation to recognize as the principal modes of accommodation appropriate for a university community of scholars."[18]

The AFT, on the other hand, believes that college faculties should resort to collective bargaining to advance their interests, and if necessary, should strike. Said Kugler: "Collective bargaining provides negotiations under conditions of equality between the trustees-administrators and the teaching staff. The cant and hypocrisy of all sorts of advisory intramural faculty committees, senates, and councils are swept away and real negotiations can take place."[19]

After pointing out that his commitment to research and teaching provides the moral legitimacy for the professor's claim to professional autonomy, Kadish contended that collective bargaining and the strike are incompatible with the teacher's professional ideas:

> *What is involved in the regularized use of the strike in the*

> *collective bargaining relationship . . . is shifting the basis of professorial claims from common commitment and moral entitlement to the play of power in a competitive context. The move from academic senate to collective bargaining backed by the strike is a move to the marketplace, and the spirit of the marketplace is that you are entitled to what you can exact, and what you can exact is what you are entitled to.*[20]

Kadish also asserted that the strike endangers the system of governance which he believes holds the greatest promise for effective progress in research and education. "I have in mind," he said, "the potential destructiveness of the collective bargaining strike to cooperative and shared decision-making between the faculty and the administration and the governing board of the university."

Whatever one's view of unionism, collective bargaining, and the strike, he is forced to conclude, I believe, that collective bargaining will become much more common than it is today. One forecaster has predicted that "organizations of professional employees—both those which call themselves unions and those which do not—will increasingly take their ideology and their rhetoric from the general employed professional model, their goals and status aspirations from the academic model, and their tactics from the union model. . . . In brief, they will do their best to look and sound like professional societies, but, if necessary, will act more like unions."[21]

Unionism will develop unevenly among colleges and universities. It has been said that governing boards and administrations probably will get the kind of professional relations and organizations they deserve. It is significant that the greatest growth of unionism and collective bargaining seems to be taking place in junior colleges and multipurpose public colleges and universities which, as former teachers colleges, have had a tradition of administrative domination and niggardly faculty participation. Unionism will also develop rapidly in institutions whose governing boards chronically interfere with the normal processes of internal governance, especially the faculty's control over its own membership and over the curriculum. It was said, for example, that the membership of the AFT local at Berkeley increased greatly after the Board of Regents withdrew the authority it had previously delegated to the campuses to appoint and promote members of the faculty.

Even in institutions which escape unionism and collective bargaining for a time, the spirit of confrontation will intensify. Students are unlikely to moderate their demands. Lunsford has sketched what we may expect:

> *We have entered a turbulent period of explicit "status politics," in the university, as students press for delineation of status rights to go with their obligations for social conformity. The changes wrought already have been great, but the costs also have been great—including major disruptions for great universities and jail terms, fines, and stunted careers for many talented and highly moral young people. The process shows few signs of stopping now; the contending parties are too far apart on the terms in which a discourse might be held. Many painful accommodations and compromises remain to be made, and it can only be hoped that the costs on both sides will soon lessen.*[22]

Faculty members also, especially in institutions with traditions of strict surveillance by governing boards and of overriding administrative authority, may be expected to challenge trustees and administrators and to assert and demand their own autonomy. Their attitude generally is that administrators cannot administer an educational institution effectively unless they are fully responsible to the entire academic community, that is, the faculty and students.

Throughout the struggle for power and influence, the competing parties will often disregard the fundamental fact of social accountability. But the public will assert its interests in higher education and will do so sharply if these interests are repeatedly ignored or challenged. The president of the American Council on Education said recently that "whatever the responses of institutions to demands for change, those responses must take into account the fact that colleges and universities are created and maintained for the good of the larger society, and not just for the benefit of those directly connected with them." He went on, "This generalization holds for students and professors no less than for administrators and trustees."[23] The intimate relationships between higher education and society have also been emphasized recently by the chairman of the Carnegie Commission on the Future of Higher Education.

> *The role of higher education becomes ever more crucial to growth, as it does for the achievement of equality of opportunity, improved health care, and the general political and cultural welfare of the nation. Higher education, as Woodrow Wilson once said at Princeton, is in the "nation's service." . . . The corollary of being in the service of the nation is that the nation has wishes about how it should be served. From religion to science, from agriculture to health, from depression to interplanetary probes, the nation has made its wishes known and higher education has obliged.*[24]

As they expand their financial support, the nation and the state will make institutions responsible for applying public funds to the purposes for which they were requested or received and, in the long run, will hold them accountable for the efficiency with which the money is used. If one were to ask faculty members, even in tax-supported institutions, whether they considered themselves publicly accountable, many of them would reply, "Certainly not." Students would probably be even more disdainful of the public interest. The report of the Berkeley Commission on University Governance was indicative of this attitude. The state legislature was mentioned only once, and nowhere in the document was the subject of broad public accountability mentioned, much less discussed. University autonomy was assumed.

The British universities have the strongest tradition of autonomy. But they, too, are in the public service and so they have become increasingly responsible for serving national goals, manpower needs, and educational priorities. Their public responsibility and vulnerability have been intensified as they have become increasingly dependent on the state for financial support. The government is exercising increasing surveillance over the way in which the universities are using public funds. As a result, they have become more and more fearful of losing their independence and of being subjected to much greater governmental intervention. In fact, such intervention has grown steadily, although the University Grants Committee (UGC), which is the intermediary between the government and the universities, has screened much of it from the public view. Under pressure from the Department of Education and Science, the UGC is becoming more directive. Traditionally, the committee, once it received its state appropriation, made "block" grants to the universities (supplemented by a limited number of "earmarked" allocations) which they were permitted to distribute internally largely as they chose.

Recently, however, the UGC has become much more explicit about the purposes for which grants are to be used. In announcing its university allocations under the quinquennial grant for 1967–1972, the committee for the first time sent the universities a memorandum of general guidance. This letter stated that the major increases in enrollment must be in the number of students in the arts rather than the sciences, that the number of postgraduate students for which the committee had provided was considerably smaller than the universities had wished, that postgraduate studies should be shifted from the more traditional courses to those which are more vocational and shorter in duration, that the universities should cooperate much more closely with industry, and that there should be much greater collaboration among the universities and between the universities and other sectors of higher education. The committee recently announced that not more than 35 per cent of the members of the academic staff could hold appointments at the level of senior lecturer and above. Under what one suspects was prodding from the ministry, the UGC some time ago began a series of cost studies in the universities, and took steps to reduce the range of unit costs in specified fields among the institutions. These are but examples of greater direction of university affairs.

In 1967, for the first time, the UGC, in making its grants to the institutions, sent each a letter of intent, stating the bases on which the committee had computed its allocations. In the case of Oxford, for example, the letter specified the number of science students, students in other subjects, and postgraduate students on which the university's allocation had been made. It also stated the sums which it had had in mind for strengthening instruction in specified fields and noted the items in the university's request for which the committee had made no provision.

Presumably the UGC does not demand that the universities follow the specifications in the letter of intent. No one has any very clear idea of what retribution might follow if an institution failed to do so. To date, apparently, no institution has decided to make a major challenge of the committee's and the government's authority.

The British universities have suffered a still greater governmental incursion. Until very recently, the accounts of the universities have been open to the University Grants Committee, but not to Parliament. Now, however, the Public Accounts Committee of Parliament and the comptroller and auditor general have begun to inspect the universities' accounts. The comptroller has assured the UGC and the universities that he and his staff will not raise questions concerning educational policy. It is difficult to see, of course, how it will be possible to appraise the effectiveness of financial administration without considering the purposes for which funds are expended. It seems almost inevitable that academic policy will come under parliamentary committee review. Since universities in the United States are used to postaudits, they would not particularly fear the financial review to which the British institutions are now being subjected. But, in Britain, the inspection of university accounts presages a period of much more direct and detailed accountability to the state. Michael Beloff said recently that universities, "whether academics like it or not, have become community projects. They are financed overwhelmingly by public money. Their growth, even their creation, has been dictated by social pressures and not the demands of scholastic independence. And therefore the time has come to acknowledge that internal debate alone cannot settle the priority of a university's function."[25]

The trend here and in Britain, then, is for universities and colleges to become instruments of public policy in even greater degree. Presumably their governing boards should play a key role in sensitizing these institutions to their public responsibilities, while at the same time protecting and enhancing their intellectual freedom. Ideally, governing boards should function as intermediaries between the outside world and the institutions they serve. Their responsibility is to represent the interests of the public at large to the academic community, and vice versa. With few exceptions, the governing boards of American institutions are composed of lay members, except that presidents sometimes serve ex officio, and fairly frequently now faculty members sit on the governing bodies of institutions other than their own. However, there are only a few instances in which faculty serve as trustees of their own college or university.

In some universities, student activists and some faculty members have attacked the principle of lay governance and have vented their wrath and disapproval on particular boards of trustees. They have charged that trustees represent privilege and power, and not the broad interests of a pluralistic society; that trustees would, if they could, restrict the academic freedom of faculty members and students; that they still think that going to college should be a privilege and not a right; that they favor a hierarchical system of government and administration in which decisions are made at the top and imposed down the line; and that they continually interfere in matters which faculty or students, or faculty and students, should control.

Studies of the composition of governing boards and the attitudes of their members give some credence to these charges, although there is a great deal of diversity from board to board and member to member (see Chapter Two). However, it should be noted that the studies report trustees' professed attitudes, not their actions. Lazarsfeld and Thielens reported in 1958 that trustees and regents as well as administrators of colleges and universities of superior quality supported the academic freedom of social science faculties. The authors explained their finding by saying that both trustees and administrators were jealous of their institutions' prestige and academic standing, and, however conservative their own attitudes, wished to attract and hold a highly respected staff. This proved to have been true even in critical periods in which faculty members had come under aggressive conservative attack.[26] The recent studies of trustees' attitudes should now be followed by studies of trustees' behavior, in order to determine how they act in crises concerning issues of academic freedom, faculty and student participation in governance, campus control of educational policy and program, and the faculty's prerogatives with respect to its own membership.

It should be remembered that the Lazarsfeld and Thielens finding was for institutions of high quality. Generally speaking, it is probable that institutions of lesser academic distinction have not enjoyed the same protection. Unfortunately, there are exceptions to the tendency for trustees to protect prestigious institutions from political interference or public pressure. For example, critics have charged that the regents of the University of California have sometimes served as a conduit for political intervention rather than as a buffer against it. The Berkeley Academic Senate Policy Committee recently declared that instead of protecting the university against the whims of the public mind, the regents' actions of late have been "decided by the latest results of the latest poll of public opinion." Unfortunately, the ex officio membership of the governor, the lieutenant governor, and the speaker of the assembly on the Board of Regents of the University of California opens the board to direct political interference.

Galbraith has called the whole concept of lay governance into question. He has declared that lay trustees really do not govern major universities any longer, and in fact are incapable of doing so. It is the faculty which now governs, and only the faculty can govern. He has pointed out that whereas once the influential lay trustee was necessary to the university, the university is now necessary to the business tycoon who is the typical trustee and to the industrial society which he represents. In fact, colleges and universities are essential to all the enterprises of society—social, political, economic, and cultural. Galbraith believes that in order to serve social interests without becoming subservient to any of them, the university must maintain its autonomy and that it can only if the faculty governs it (with some assistance from students and other elements of the university complex).[27]

Is lay governance anachronistic? I believe that governing boards composed exclusively of laymen are no longer adequate to the task of governing colleges and universities, large or small. Before proposing an alternative, however, one should consider the functions which laymen have performed and still may be able to perform in building bridges between institutions and society. It should be instructive to look at the British experience.

The faculties of Oxford and Cambridge are self-governing societies. "They are," said Robbins, "syndicalist organizations—pure examples of producers' democracy. There are no representatives of the public as such concerned with, or responsible for, their ultimate decisions."[28] It is interesting—and perhaps significant—that when the civic universities emerged in the nineteenth century, none of them followed the Oxbridge model. The conditions under which the Red Brick universities were established made the imitation of Oxford and Cambridge inappropriate. The former originated as teaching institutions sponsored by local people who hired the teachers and admitted the students. "It was natural, therefore," said Sydney Caine, "that when they attained university status it was a non-academic group, composed largely of representatives of local government authorities and other local organizations which emerged as the effective executive authority." Caine went on, "The standard constitution of the new universities . . . provided for a council with a majority of such lay members but with some academic representation, controlling finance and, in form at least, appointments; and a senate, entirely academic in composition, dealing with 'academic' matters."[29]

It is significant, however, that the new universities established after the war have all followed the Red Brick tradition by establishing governing bodies composed of both lay members and faculty representatives. This certainly suggests that the British universities have found lay participation in governance to be helpful. What functions, then, do they think the laymen have performed?

Robbins believed that Oxford and Cambridge would be much stronger institutions if laymen participated in their government. Speaking to the point at Oxford, he said:

> *My intention was certainly not to suggest that in the outside world there could conceivably be people more eminent than there are actually in this university. But eminence is not what is the prime desideratum in this connection: it is rather a certain degree of independence, of not being im-*

mediately concerned in one's private life in the effects of the various decisions which are taken; and for that purpose the cooperation even of people with comparatively humble intellectual equipment, provided they have some moral standing, is sometimes of considerable assistance.[30]

The report of the Committee on Higher Education, which was chaired by Robbins, rationalized the participation of laymen in governing bodies as follows:

More than 85 per cent of university finance comes from public sources and in our judgment it is in general neither practicable nor justifiable that the spending of university funds should be wholly in the hands of the users. Academic autonomy is more likely to be safeguarded where the public has a guarantee that there is independent lay advice and criticism within the university. . . . Where men and women of wide experience and high standing in the world of affairs can spare time to associate themselves with university activities, the universities gain from the partnership strength and sagacity in their dealings with the outside world. And, even where academic affairs are concerned, lay arbitration is a valuable resource in case of conflict.[31]

It is the membership of academics on governing bodies that has distinguished the British from the American universities. Robbins takes the presence of faculty members on university councils for granted. In the report of the Committee on Higher Education and in subsequent presentations, Robbins considered it necessary to justify lay members rather than to comment on the necessity of faculty representation. Over time, however, the balance of influence between the academics and the public representatives has changed. Caine has summarized the transition as follows: "Over the years the influence of the academics has increased, through the advice given by the senate and through the part played in the council by its academic members, inevitably more expert and more continuously involved than the average lay member. All the universities have tended therefore to move, so far as detailed administration is concerned, in the direction of full academic self-government." Caine pointed out that the academic members and academic senates have increased their power at the expense of the laymen, and that this trend is likely to continue: "Even in London, the net effect of various recent changes, in working arrangements rather than in constitutional provision, is to increase the power of the teachers of the university, including at least some move towards giving them greater influence in broad financial policy."[32]

As in the United States, senate membership in the British universities is concentrated in the senior grades of staff. Recently, however, there has been increasing pressure for participation by faculty members at junior ranks, as there has also been increasing pressure for student participation not only in senates but also in the governing councils.

In the changing balance of power and influence in British higher education, it is the third party—the government—which has gained at the expense of laymen and academics. Caine has observed that many of the policies which have formerly been decided by university councils are now determined at the central government level, largely by the Department of Education and Science and the University Grants Committee. He also predicted that the effective share of government in controlling university policy would increase and that the power of the faculties would continue to grow, even to the point of exercising greater influence in financial policy, which has been the traditional prerogative of the councils.

Faculty power may be curbed in other ways, however. Academic decisions will increasingly have to be taken according to guidelines established by the government through the University Grants Committee. Thus, the power of central agencies will grow at the expense both of lay members and of faculty representatives on governing bodies. Caine concluded that however the balance of power may shift, the two centers of influence will be the government and the faculties, tempered, I would add, by increasing pressure for student participation. The score card on who gains and who loses will have to be revised periodically, as will the countdown on shifting patterns of cooperation and competition in controlling university affairs.

The time has come in American higher education to rearrange patterns of authority. First, boards of trustees should no longer be confined mainly to those who represent wealth, position, or political power. Even the public university has responded primarily in the past to the articulate, the influential, and the powerful in society. It must now become responsive to a wider range of economic interests, and to a pluralistic political constituency, as well as to a more diverse pattern of ethnic and cultural backgrounds and aspirations.

Second, governing boards should include a substantial proportion of faculty representatives. Faculties quite rightly will not accept token representation. One or two faculty members in a rather large governing board, however conscientious they may be, will find it difficult to express the interests of a diverse constituency or to wield much power when critical decisions are made. Here again, the British precedent may be instructive. As of 1962, according to the Robbins Committee Report, the proportion of senate representatives on university councils ranged roughly from something less than one-fifth to approximately one-third. When the colleges of advanced technology secured university charters, they followed the precedent of joint lay-faculty council membership. For example, out of thirty-six members, the council of the new University of Aston in Birmingham includes nine members of the university faculty or staff. In American universities and colleges, it would seem appropriate for faculty representatives to constitute from a fourth to a third of the voting members.

Furthermore, either student representatives should become voting members of governing boards, or formal arrangements should be made for continuing substantial student representation at meetings of the board and its committees. To supplement formal association of students and faculty members with governing boards, there should be numerous opportunities for joint discussion of college and university affairs among trustees, administrative officers, faculty members, students, alumni, and other constituencies. To this end, either formal councils should be established or special task forces should be created, or both. No group should have absolute power, although for purposes of orderly administration, responsibility for final decisions should be clearly defined. These decisions should be the culmination of widespread participation.

In the United States, as in Britain, the distribution of authority, power, and influence is in flux and will be for the indeterminate future. Individual faculty members have gained greatly through access to external sources of funds. Not only have they become more independent of administrative authority and influence, but they have gained autonomy at the expense of the corporate faculty as well. In institutions which have been ruled primarily by governing boards and administrative officers, faculty power may be expected to grow.

However, in institutions where the faculty has gained a large degree of authority and influence, it may lose no small part of its control. In large and complex universities whose support flows from many sources and in which there will be increasing internal and external pressure for efficient management, faculties may lose whatever influence over the allocation of resources and detailed budgeting they may previously have won. At Berkeley, for example, the Senate Budget Committee, which once kept line items under surveillance, now deals only broadly with budget policy and has little influence over the allocation of resources. The chancellor's office has increased its budgetary control simply because, in detail and in complexity, it has become unmanageable by the Senate Budget Committee.

Faculties will be increasingly frustrated in academic planning and administration as educational decisions are more and more made by external agencies. Institutions which are members of systems such as the California state colleges or groups of state universities in Illinois find themselves constrained by remote systemwide governing boards and by the policies and practices of distant central administrations. Faculties in particular institutions are limited in their authority to introduce new curricula, develop graduate studies, or expand research activities.

Whole systems may be constrained by superboards such as the Ohio Board of Regents and the Illinois Board of Higher Education. Scarce resources and expanding social demands seem to require concerted planning and coordination among both public and private colleges and universities. Often the purpose of coordination is to fit particular institutions into a grand plan, in which functions and programs are allocated and assigned by superior governing or coordinating bodies or both. In coordinated systems, institutional autonomy is inevitably to some degree sacrificed on the altar of efficiency. In some instances, statewide master plans fasten a relatively inflexible pattern on higher education which thwarts the desirable evolution of particular campuses or groups of institutions.

Frustrated by all these impediments, faculties may become increasingly contentious and resistive to both internal and external constraints. The redistribution of power in higher education will not proceed smoothly or amicably; it will be accompanied by turbulence, controversy, and even conflict. The resolution of conflicting forces and purposes will be beyond the capability of any one faculty or administration, any one institution, any system, or any state. It will call for statesmanship of a high order, leadership capable of mobilizing the efforts of all who have a stake in the maintenance of intellectual freedom in the university and in the society.

References

[1] M. Bundy, "Faculty Power," *Atlantic Monthly,* September 1968, pp. 41–47.

[2] *Ibid.*

[3] B. Clark, "Faculty Authority," *AAUP Bulletin,* Winter 1961, pp. 293–302.

[4] C. Foote, H. Mayer, and Associates, *The Culture of the University: Governance and Education* (San Francisco: Jossey-Bass, 1968), pp. 32–33.

[5] R. Eckert, "Participation in University Policy-Making: A Second Look" (Minneapolis: University of Minnesota, mimeographed tentative draft). Also W. Deegan and K. Mortimer, "Faculty Government at the University of Minnesota" (Berkeley: University of California, Center for Research and Development in Higher Education, 1969, tentative draft).

[6] W. Deegan, T. McConnell, K. Mortimer, and H. Stull, "Joint Participation in Decision-Making" (Berkeley: University of California, Center for Research and Development in Higher Education, May 1969).

[7] K. Mortimer, *Academic Government at Berkeley: The Academic Senate* (Ph.D. Dissertation, University of California, Berkeley, 1969).

[8] Mortimer, *op. cit.*

[9] Foote, Mayer, and Associates, *op. cit.*, p. 32.

[10] Eckert, *op. cit.*

[11] Deegan, McConnell, Mortimer, and Stull, *op. cit.*

[12] Foote, Mayer, and Associates, *op. cit.*, p. 99.

[13] T. Lunsford, "Authority and Ideology in the Administered University," *American Behavioral Scientist,* May-June 1968, pp. 5–14.

[14] E. Gross, and P. Grambsch, *University Goals and Academic Power* (Washington, D.C.: American Council on Education, 1968), pp. 107–115.

[15] Foote, Mayer, and Associates, *op. cit.*, p. 17.

[16] C. Byse, "Collective Bargaining and Unionism in American Higher Education: Some Preliminary Comments," address delivered at the Danforth Foundation Workshop on Liberal Arts Education, Colorado Springs, Colorado (Mimeo.).

[17] I. Kugler, *AAUP and AFT—Which Way for the Professors?* Reprinted and revised from *Changing Education* (Washington, D.C.: American Federation of Teachers, n.d.).

[18] S. Kadish, "The Strike and the Professoriat," *AAUP Bulletin,* June 1968, pp. 160–168.

[19] Kugler, *op. cit.*

[20] Kadish, *op. cit.*

[21] J. Garbarino, "Professional Negotiations in Education," *Industrial Relations,* February 1968, pp. 93–106.

[22] T. Lunsford, "Who Are Members of the University Community?" *Denver Law Journal,* 1968, *45*(4), pp. 545–557.

[23] L. Wilson, "Changing University Governance: Part II," Montgomery Lecture Series, University of Nebraska, May 3, 1969 (Mimeo.).

[24] C. Kerr, *New Challenges to the College and University* (Berkeley: Carnegie Commission on Higher Education, 1969).

[25] M. Beloff, *The Plateglass Universities* (London: Secker and Warburg, 1968), p. 188.

[26] P. Lazarsfeld and W. Thielens, Jr., *The Academic Mind* (Glencoe, Ill.: Free Press, 1958), pp. 159–191.

[27] J. Galbraith, *The New Industrial State* (Boston: Houghton Mifflin, 1967), pp. 370–378.

[28] Lord Robbins, *The University in the Modern World* (London: Macmillan, 1966), p. 69.

[29] Sir S. Caine, *British Universities: Purpose and Prospects* (London: The Bodley Head, 1969), pp. 155–156.
[30] Robbins, *op. cit.*, p. 82.
[31] Committee on Higher Education, *Higher Education* (London: Her Majesty's Stationery Office, 1963), p. 218.
[32] Caine, *op. cit.*, pp. 156, 159.

8

Ray A. Howe

Roles of Faculty

In his 1968 annual report, published only a few months prior to the dramatic outbreak that occurred on the campus over which he presides, Nathan Pusey of Harvard offered the following observation: "The ivory tower has become a laughably grotesque symbol of the contemporary institution of higher learning. What do we do in such troubled circumstances as we are now experiencing? I suspect the path of prudence for those of us in positions of responsibility for academic institutions is simply to stay alert, to keep mindful of our distant goals, and in a tumultuous sea, to navigate as best we can."[1]

This is small comfort, indeed, whatever the soundness of the advice, and small wonder the small comfort. Collegiate administrators today are being required to face situations for which neither training not experience, neither aptitude nor inclination does anything to prepare them. They are confronted with, if nothing worse, the necessity of recognizing the wisdom of Abraham Lincoln's advice, given over a century ago, to the effect that the dogmas of the quiet past are inadequate for the stormy present, and that we must disenthrall ourselves and think anew. Perhaps there is nothing worse than this particular type of confrontation, the confrontation with a changing reality. Yet we might do well to ponder the significance of Lincoln's advice, for it does appear that time-honored methods of resolution of institutional stresses in higher education have, in many instances, fallen short not of perfection but of minimal effectiveness.

Disenthrallment, ridding oneself of a slavish servitude, is not an easy task. It is trying, perhaps even traumatic. Eric Hoffer, viewing the dimensions of change, has offered this perceptive generalization, which may have very particular application in higher education:

> *We can never be really prepared for that which is wholly new. We have to adjust ourselves, and every radical adjustment is a crisis in self-esteem; we undergo a test, we have to prove ourselves. It needs inordinate self-confidence to face drastic change without inner trembling. The simple fact that we can never be fit and ready for that which is wholly new has some peculiar results. It means that a population undergoing drastic change is a population of misfits and breathes in an atmosphere of passion. There is a close connection between lack of confidence and the passionate state of mind and . . . passionate intensity may serve as a substitute for confidence.*[2]

The first productive, educative step may well be the dispelling of certain preconceptions, which, although they may once have conformed to the data, today may not.

There is no need to trace the evolution, or revolution at times, of the emerging patterns of faculty-administrative relationships. It is difficult to generalize historically with any precision and even more difficult to know what broad statements are applicable today. We could note that there has developed a recognizable bureaucratic hierarchy of administration, which can be represented in a diagram in the form of a triangle, more isosceles than equilateral.

Resting precariously atop the apex of this triangle—or, more properly, this pyramid—and touching it at only one point, is the board of trustees. The point at which the board touches is, of course, the presidency. Beneath the apex, in ever-widening layers of fat, lie the varying and ever-increasing substrata of administration. Somewhere in the mass, appropriately obscure yet gratifyingly apparent, is the academic dean.

Weaving its way through this pyramid are channels of communication. Sometimes they are called chains of command, but not in educational circles. To many faculty members such channels seem, however unintentionally, ingeniously constructed to serve two functions: to delay, alter, emasculate, diffuse, divert or blunt any missive emanating from the nether regions; yet simultaneously, in some mysterious legerdemain, to accelerate, expedite, substantiate, even hopefully authenticate such pearls of wisdom as may be either hurled or casually dropped from the Olympian heights, which, the laws of falling bodies being what they are, tend to splatter when they hit, having consequently a more negative than positive acceptance.

Anyone attempting to examine the patterns of faculty-administrative relationships must admit that we have, at best, a tangled web, though it remains for individual judgment to determine whether this is, in fact, the "tangled web we weave when first we practice to deceive." We have departments and divisions, programs and centers, studies and schools, projects and operations, and God knows what else, for each of which we have somewhere a conceivable combination of head, chairman, director, coordinator, dean, chancellor, provost, or what have you. The greatest irony may lie in our attempts to organize on a "discipline" basis—or, even more so, on an interdisciplinary basis. What results may be structure, but it suggests chaos. Yet each individual in the college has a place in the diagram.

Next we have the faculty committee structure, both standing and ad hoc. This is the arena in which it is commonly alleged that we "keep minutes and waste hours." These committees are, theoretically at least, related to functions and the origins of each can, however nominally, be traced to such a source; yet the need for their preservation or persistence is questionable. Like most of us, they tend to outlive their administrative usefulness, sometimes perpetuated for no reason more apparent than to allow each aspiring bureaucrat-to-be another entry in his vita.

Then comes the organization of the faculty apart from but appropriate to the institutional administrative function. The disciplinary societies, and the interdisciplinary organizations, which, in respect to their continuing and enduring nature, are like the still broader institutions, the American Association of University Professors, the American Council on Education, the American Association of Junior Colleges, the American Association for Higher Education, and whatever hybrid the National Education Association may create in the current reorganization. Beyond these lie those exercises in group therapy or sensitivity training, the conferences, the workshops, the symposia, and the institutes, and, finally, the Faculty Senate. One of the prime factors in the evaluation of the viability of faculty in an institution has been, traditionally, the existence of or provision for such an organization. This accomplished, it was hoped that the resulting confused condition would somehow allow each faculty member to pursue his interest and his expertise individually without restraint; and from this arrangement the individual student, the institution, and the greater society were to benefit immeasurably.

One could well argue that the faculty is organized to a fault—and it *is,* because, in increasing numbers, faculty members perceive that the outcomes of such overorganization, if not the intent, have been to concentrate rather than to diffuse power and to make the faculty an instrument of the board and administration rather than the converse—which is what, so faculty tradition holds, the university or college operation is all about.

Two developments have become increasingly obvious: criticisms of the existing order of things, once covert, have become recognizably overt, and from highly respectable sources; and higher education faculties have become demonstrably interested in the phenomenon of collective bargaining, as a consequence, perhaps, of their appraisal of its course and consequences in the lower echelons of education. Both of these tendencies seem likely to grow. Others not yet apparent may well emerge with increasing student unrest. This evidence of faculty malaise bids fair to revolutionize our lives in many ways.

There is an obvious and logical question: Why? Why, when in the words of Arnold Weber, who headed the AAHE Task Force a few years ago, "it is apparent to even the most monastic academic that he probably never had it so good." The Task Force itself provided an answer: "Faculty dissatisfaction is clearly a child of growth and affluence."[3]

It is readily understandable how factors of growth could cause new tensions and aggravate old. But the affluence aspect may be too little appreciated. Crane Brinton advanced the idea, which social history now seems to reinforce, that social resolution is not an outreach from deprivation, but rather the outcome of a period of increasing affluence for those who undertake the revolution.[4] They acquire a modest sense of well-being and then seem to acquire the realization that they are worthy of much more, coupled with the recognition that they have already secured the base from which they may reasonably hope to achieve it. In Weber's words, these aspirations take the form of the demand for "the full prerogatives of professionalism. This means that professors, like members of other professions, seek direct participation in the formulation of the policies and rules that govern their performance."[5] The key word here is *direct*.

Higher education today must be recognized, in business terms, as a major growth industry and it is not at all surprising, it is almost predictable, that this phenomenon should be accompanied by the "revolution of rising expectations" which has become so characteristic of numerous other elements of society in the twentieth century. Other groups have discovered that automatic and gratuitous fulfillment does not go hand in hand with the mere rise in expectations. They have learned, and by example taught, that it must be reached for, even fought for. As Cass and Birnbaum point out, "Many occupational groups in America have learned that it is not the justice of individual demands that wins increased salaries and higher status from society, but the economic and political power or organized groups."[6] But Cass and Birnbaum feature something which is not given prime importance in most other quarters. They point out that society's ambivalent attitude toward the profession, perhaps coupled with the teachers' own traditional feeling of self-doubt, or—in the social psychologist's term—self-hate, have created an environment in which "teachers have been undergoing a process of progressive alienation both from the school as an institution and from the community it serves."[7]

It has long been recognized by most of those in the field that there has been a sense of alienation of teaching faculty from administration, and perhaps even vice versa; it may be characterized as a kind of cold war of long standing, and it is now becoming increasingly hot. Of course, the radical change in our society serves only to accentuate the tension. If conflict-reducing and tension-relieving mechanisms are either necessary or desirable why can we not call upon the traditional mechanisms and expect, reasonably and confidently, that they will suffice? This was the first, predictable reaction to the spector of collective bargaining especially evident in the community college. John Livingston, long an active participant in the California faculty senate movement, warned, "Those who will not share their power willingly are likely to share it unwillingly—across the bargaining table, and with a professorial union."[8] Others have gone further to declare categorically that where collective bargaining appears, the college president stands condemned of not having treated the faculty as faculty. This argument suggests that the emergence of collective bargaining is not the beginning of a time of trial but the end of one, and an ending with an automatic verdict of guilty. Small wonder that academic officers view this change, in Eric Hoffer's words, as "a crisis in self-esteem."

But Livingston takes a more analytic view and he finds some weakness in the faculty senate:

It is important to note here that the traditional structure

> *of higher educational institutions virtually ensures that the faculty will be represented on campus government as members of interest groups rather than as acting, choosing, deliberating members of a common enterprise. Insofar as campus government follows the administrative organization of the institution into departments, divisions, and schools based on the academic disciplines, the result will be a senate which is a legislature composed of the lobbyists themselves. The ordinary political process in America is dominated by the accommodation of group interests despite the fact that its geographic constituencies represent citizens. Little imagination is needed to see the consequences of making the interests themselves the constituencies.*[9]

Let it be understood that even if faculty opt for a faculty senate as the proper vehicle for their reach for power, Livingston strongly suggests that academic deans may be working with faculty along avenues, even alleys, not the lanes of power, and that the traditional routes of curricular development and change may be apart from, even divorced from, the decision-making process of the institution insofar as it involves faculty. Livingston, burdened with doubts as to the viability of the outcome he foresees, still feels obliged to pronounce, "We seem destined, in short, to move increasingly toward relationships of an adversary type, characterized by confrontation and bargaining, backed by force, by threat and intimidation." He sees one glimmer of hope: "An academic senate seems to pose the best chance for defining collective negotiations in flexible ways and for keeping alive the idea that bargaining is a second-best alternative to which, unfortunately, events have forced us."[10]

This hope may be dim. Weber's report makes this point. "We do not preclude the possibility of a constructive coexistence between an academic senate and a bargaining agency, but the long-run prospects must be rated as slim. By selecting a bargaining agent, a majority of the faculty members have chosen to emphasize their employee status and implicit power in their dealings with the administration. Under these circumstances it is extremely difficult to sustain the notion of 'shared authority' that must underlie an effective academic senate."[11] Weber, individually, later said after one year's experience, "Where a union comes in the deal is off as far as the senate is concerned."[12]

Yet another critical view of faculty senates may offer some illumination of problems as well as some gloom in respect to prospects. Myron Lieberman expounded the inadequacy of faculty senates in respect to personnel considerations and their effective representation. His views are studied, documented, and well argued. His primary point is made in his concluding remarks: "One of our crucial needs in higher education is an end to the uncritical approach to faculty self-government, especially to faculty senates. Most discussion on these topics is characterized by ready resort to theological incantations instead of data. . . . A day of reckoning for faculty senates is close at hand in many institutions." Lieberman also stated rather bluntly, "As far as being the mechanism for representing faculties on terms and conditions of employment, I think their future is behind them."[13] Bleak prospects, indeed, for faculty senates. Dread prospects, indeed, for those who fear the coming of collective bargaining.

Academic deans may incline to find some sense of security in their certainty, which is largely the by-product of self-assurance, that curriculum and related matters are not proper or appropriate items for negotiations. Only a short time ago it was said with similar conviction that collective bargaining was simply not applicable to any level of education. That illusion seems shattered. Other illusions will follow in short order. For the truth is that what is or is not negotiable is, of itself, negotiable. In other words, you must bargain about what you will bargain about. In the specific instance of curriculum, can it not be readily grasped how curriculum matters can be easily construed to be, in one sense, "working conditions," which are clearly, under the most conservative interpretation, subject to collective bargaining?

Collective bargaining will come only when and if the faculty asks for it and, in those increasing number of states where enabling legislation has been enacted, it must come if faculty so choose. The fundamental burden of collective bargaining, then, is the fact that administrators must adapt to collective bargaining without any compensatory reciprocal requirement, indeed no requirement at all, that collective bargaining adapt to administrators. Redundant as it may seem, collective bargaining simply cannot be imposed on faculty collectively; it can be imposed only on administrators collectively. If they invoke collective bargaining, faculty members do have to make adjustments, some of which they have proved extremely reluctant to face. There is simply no escaping this fact. It is far better for all concerned if such adjustments are made straightforwardly and without reservation. All people confronted with collective bargaining would then know precisely where they stand and they could seek advice and assistance to enable them to do so more intelligently and capably.

To invoke collective bargaining may, however innocently, invite disaster. Collective bargaining establishes a power relationship. Power is difficult enough to deal with if one is ever conscious of its presence. It is not an amateur's plaything. Any attempt at a relationship which, consciously or unconsciously, even momentarily sets aside the realization that the power is there could lead to confusion, even chaos, should the power be suddenly, albeit inadvertently, "turned on." When collective bargaining comes, the administrator has a greater adjustment to make than does the faculty member. The administrator may find himself in the unwelcome position of the groom at a shotgun wedding: he may be there as a consequence of his own activity, but not by his own choice. However, it is incumbent on the administrator to adopt a positive attitude, not simply an open mind, toward collective bargaining. A positive attitude will not ensure positive outcomes, but its *absence* will go far to ensure negative outcomes. Social psychologists have had a great deal to say about this phenomenon. One is cast in an adversary relationship, but one can be a determined and vigorous adversary, where conviction or circumstance seems to require it, without being a hostile antagonist of anybody or anything. The latter is an exercised option, and must be recognized as such.

The major distinction between the processes inherent in collective bargaining and those more attributable to a collegial relationship is the pursuit of compromise as opposed to consensus. Our primary difficulty may be that one of these is endowed with a noble connotation while the other tends to be regarded as ignoble in its manifestations. These are value judgments which may or may not have any validity. And certainly it must be said that value judgments are made, not in a vacuum, but in a context, and may well change with a varying context. It is worthy of consideration that compromise might be as stable and as intelligent a solution as consensus, perhaps even more so.

In our day faculty members need no external stimulus to organize themselves to relate to administration save that provided by the temper of the times. Faculty *may* desire an alternative to their current course, but if such an alternative is to have any hope of acceptance it must possess two basic characteristics: strong organization and direct group action. No substitutes for these characteristics are likely to be allowed. Currently unionlike pursuits offer them, and faculty body after faculty body is finding it relatively, often amazingly, easy to turn its back on the image of professionalism in favor of the reality of power.

Administrators seem now almost eager, certainly ready, to talk to faculty about "shared authority," the phrase so dear to the AAUP. Yet in doing so administrators seem painfully reluctant to face what shared authority has always implied: a balance of power. No mechanism is more ideally suited to provide the opportunity for a balance of power than is collective bargaining; but it does not assure a balance of power. Instance after instance of negotiations reliably confirms this. Usually the absence of such a balance is the error of omission on the part of administration. Through ignorance, indifference, indecision, or downright ineptitude administration often fails to bring its power to the table. Its ultimate power is to refuse to be coerced.

The tragedy of such an error of omission is that when it occurs the potential of collective bargaining is consequently unrealized. Not unless there is a balance of power at the table are the participants required to reach beyond coercion to creative, constructive, and cooperative ventures to resolve the problems before them.

The success or failure of such a project is, to an almost immeasurable degree, dependent on the quality of the persons responsible for the bargaining—on both sides of the table. Bargaining, like other complex human relations, is an art at least as much as it is a skill. So, however, is the construction of a continuing and reasonably secure relationship within the context of a faculty senate —and here the relationship's continuity is at least in part dependent on the whim of the administration or board. In the bargaining process however, the option is with the faculty.

The life of the institution is in jeopardy not so much in consequence of the form faculty militancy may take, as in consequence of the response to the form faculty militancy adopts. In faculty unrest, as in student unrest, the most basic question is not why some are radical, but rather why those radical individuals find broad acceptance among their nonradical associates. The AAHE Task Force said it, even as they opted otherwise:

> *Although we have a clear preference for the establishment of a strong independent faculty senate, we do not view the arrival of unions* qua *unions on the campus as a major threat to the fundamental nature of institutions of higher education. When a bargaining agency has gained representation rights for the faculty, the appropriate task is to promote a relationship that will best realize the potential benefits of this new arrangement and minimize the costs. . . . The record of experience in the industrial sector in the United States indicates that unions have been able to adapt their policies to the special conditions of their environment,* and to make constructive contributions to the administration of an enterprise. Such contributions are not likely to be forthcoming, however, when management adopts an intransigent position. [*Emphasis supplied.*][14]

It is easy to adopt an intransigent position, especially when one's preferences or biases or convictions are involved. It is, conversely, extremely difficult to attain a perspective which allows for reasonably objective analysis. In this instance it may be close to impossible; yet it must be done. Several rather fundamental considerations are becoming increasingly obvious, and deservedly so. Faculty are, in sufficient instances to constitute a trend, rejecting the traditional patterns through which supposed involvement in collegiate decision-making has been provided. This change is occurring because of both external and internal stimuli, that is, societal pressures in general and institutional pressures in particular. In the minds of faculty, the *effective* alternatives are few, indeed, if any. Any effective alternative must include two basic factors—it must be internally consistent and at the same time be relevant to the basic realities of the social context in which it takes place. Faculty seem, for the immediate future, to be vitally interested in organizing for themselves. Administration may still play a vital role, but in the implementation stage rather than the organizational stage. Administrative reaction may well be the major determinant of whether productive and contributory outcomes will emanate from such faculty reorganization as may occur. Academic administrators in particular may well be confronted with a dilemma: either their particular pursuits may be shunted into the bypasses of the decision-making channels or, conversely, they may come to occupy center stage in any confrontation resulting from reorganization. All collegiate officers would do well to educate themselves to the details and the implications of such alternatives as may be available to faculty. Administration would be well advised, and the institutions would be well served, if a sincere and deep commitment to a determined and unwavering effort were made to assure productive and contributory outcomes no matter what form the faculty movement may take.

There is a story that has a special relevance to faculty-administrative relationships. It concerns a cleric who served for many years as a missionary in the subarctic tundra, who resolved that when he retired he would devote his last years to the growing of green, living things. On retirement, however, he discovered that his meager financial resources would permit him to acquire only a rather small patch of semiarid wasteland. But he labored with love and made the desert bloom, creating in the process a veritable garden. On one occasion he was visited by a former colleague who was, of course, taken on a tour of the project, bush by bush, plant by plant, tree by tree. As the afternoon came to an end, the visitor sought desperately for just the right words through which to convey the appreciation he so fervently felt. Finally, he thought he had them. As they stood together at the gate, he took the old man's hand in his and said, "Father, it is truly a miracle what you and

God, working together, have done here." The old man nodded, but, looking back, he felt obliged to reply. "Yes," he agreed, "but, you know, you really should have seen this place when God had it all to himself."

References

[1] N. Pusey, *Harvard University: The President's Report,* 1967–1968, January 1968, p. 2.

[2] E. Hoffer, *The Ordeal of Change* (New York: Harper and Row, 1964), pp. 1–2.

[3] *Faculty Participation in Academic Governance.* Report of the AAHE Task Force on Faculty Representation and Academic Negotiations, Campus Governance Program (Washington, D.C.: American Association for Higher Education, National Education Association, 1967), p. 9.

[4] C. Brinton, *The Anatomy of Revolution* (New York: Random House, 1952), p. 264.

[5] A. Weber, "Academic Negotiations: Alternatives to Collective Bargaining." Report presented at the Planning Session at the Twenty-second National Conference on Higher Education, Chicago, March 1967, p. 2.

[6] J. Cass and M. Birnbaum, "What Makes Teachers Militant," *Saturday Review,* January 1968, p. 55.

[7] *Ibid.,* pp. 3–4.

[8] J. Livingston, "Faculty and Administrative Roles in Decision-Making." Report presented at the Twenty-third National Conference on Higher Education, Chicago, March 1968, p. 1.

[9] *Ibid.,* pp. 3–4.

[10] J. Livingston, "Academic Senate Under Fire," in G. Smith (Ed.), *Agony and Promise: Current Issues in Higher Education 1969* (San Francisco: Jossey-Bass, 1969), pp. 170–171.

[11] Weber, *op. cit.,* p. 10.

[12] A. Weber, "Academic Governance." Report presented to the Michigan Association of Colleges and Universities, p. 8.

[13] M. Lieberman, "Faculty Senates: A Dissenting View." Report presented at the Twenty-fourth National Conference on Higher Education, Chicago, March 1969, p. 10.

[14] Weber, "Academic Negotiations: Alternatives to Collective Bargaining," p. 9.

9

Harold L. Hodgkinson

The Next Decade

Any social structure is bound together by a social cement which consists of equal parts of reciprocity and trust. The degree of cohesion will be dependent upon the amount of this social cement present. The more cement, the easier it will be to enculturate the young into adult society, and the less cement the more difficult. Three quotations will set the scene:

> *It is increasingly clear that legitimate authority is declining in the modern state. In a real sense, "law and order"* is *the basic question of our day. The crisis of legitimacy has been visible for some time in just about all of the nonpolitical sectors of life—family, economy, religion, education—and*

> *is now spreading rapidly into the political realm. The gigantic and seemingly impregnable organizations that surround and dominate men in the modern states are seen by more and more people to have at their center not a vital principle of authority but a hollow space, a moral vacuum. Increasingly, among the young and the rejected, obedience is mainly a matter of lingering habit, or expediency, or necessity, but not a matter of conviction and deepest sentiment.*[1]

> *A social organism of any sort whatever, large or small, is what it is because each member proceeds to his own duty with a trust that the other members will simultaneously do theirs. A government, an army, a commercial system, a ship, a college, an athletic team, all exist on this condition without which not only is nothing achieved, but nothing is even attempted.*[2]

> [*Democracy is*] *more than a form of government; it is primarily a mode of associated living, of conjoint communicated experience. The extension in space of the number of individuals who participate in an interest so that each has to refer his own action to that of others, and to consider the actions of others to give point and direction to his own, is equivalent to the breaking down of those barriers of class, race, and national territory which kept men from perceiving the full import of their activity.*[3]

On the other hand, living in an era of declining faith in social institutions can be enormously exciting—the sky is the limit, one can think and act in a variety of styles and pursue his own goals as far as he wishes. For the individual human being, living in the declining years of the Roman Empire (low cement) must have been glorious. It is the old who prefer the stable life, and the young who seek risk, stimulation, and change. In our society, a majority of the population is under twenty-five. Until the recent declines in birth rates have an effect of the population distribution (by about 1985) we will be living in a juvenocracy, in which the value orientations of the young will dominate over those of the old. The political structure, however, will continue to be in the power of the elderly citizens, but youth will fight it at every turn and blunt its effectiveness.

Another way to look at the problem is in terms of social class. When Warner and others began the community study movement in American sociology, the dominant class pattern was pyramid shaped, with a lower class majority. Only 5 per cent were upper class, 25 per cent were middle class, and 75 per cent were lower class. At present, America is the first nation in history to achieve a middle-class majority, diamond-shaped, with roughly 10 per cent in the upper class, a whopping 70 per cent now in the middle class, and only 20 per cent in the lower class. This fact is terribly important; it indicates that a majority of Americans, of whatever age, have a high degree of affluence. At present, this affluence is used largely in the consumption of goods and services, which transcends the bounds of age. Thus the generation gap hypothesis may mask as much as it reveals, not allowing us to see the suburban housewife studying Zen, taking Yoga exercise, and smoking marijuana (a great deal of which is smoked by over-thirty suburbanites). This also suggests a general lack of potency of the so-called Protestant Ethic, by which people worked for long-term rewards rather than immediate ones and felt that personal gratification was evil and that leisure was bad ("The devil finds work for idle hands to do"). This system, based on guilt and feelings of inadequacy which force the individual to work harder, has been partially replaced by a new value system. Its outlines are somewhat hazy, but it seems to deemphasize work for its own sake and stress self-fulfillment, substituting joy for guilt, deep personal communication rather than bureaucratic superficiality, the virtues of free time used in the expression of personality, as in the arts, a renewed sense of social responsibility for the rejected. It is an aristocratic ethic, in many respects, yet its symbols are the credit card and the installment plan; it stresses the consumer role (the way in which one consumes goods is perhaps the defining attribute of personality today), but it also encourages interest in Eastern philosophy, music and art, astrology, encounter groups, and reality therapy—those activities which stress the affective side of human experience.

Some will say that this is a temporary situation, that once the war in Vietnam is over, the pendulum will begin to shift back to the more comfortable acquisitive ethic in which people work hard for money, and students work hard for grades, and faculty work hard for tenure, and administrators (being the most Protestant Ethic-oriented of all) simply work hard. I do not believe that this will happen. One of the most important factors in cultural style is the pattern of training children, and in American homes the patterns have ranged at the permissive "extreme" since the end of World War II, and there is no reversal of this trend in sight. At the same time that large sectors of the population are raging against college authorities for not controlling student activists, an astonishing increase in the use of drugs and violence has taken place at first in the high schools, and now in the junior highs—areas in which parents have full authority to stop such activity if they wish to. The following news item may be predictive of the future: "Morristown, New Jersey: The ultimate in student disorders happened here yesterday when three four-year-olds broke into their kindergarten classroom and wrecked it, splashing paint, smashing records, and scattering games. Police said they made no demands for curriculum or faculty changes, and 'they probably got spankings at home and just went in and tore up the place.' "[4]

The vociferousness with which American parents, and the United States Congress, are threatening college administrators to shape up or ship out is due perhaps to parents' own inadequacies in dealing with their own children. The campus may represent for them the last chance for conversion before adulthood, the last possibility of covering for their own errors. As one example, during my six years as dean of the college of Bard College, one parent accosted me in a hostile way at a parent reception halfway through the fall term and insulted me and the college for allowing his son to grow a beard. I recalled that the son, a freshman, had possessed the beard when he came through the orientation program, so he must have grown it at home with parental approval. "It's true that we couldn't make him shave it off," the father replied, "but that's *your* job!" Thus we echo the classic dictum of Machiavelli, "Men must be compelled to be good, or they will invariably turn out to be bad."

Part of the problem, although it is seldom made public, is that the reward system of the campus has not moved one iota toward the new ethic we have presented. The structure does seem inhuman, and seems designed to punish people and reject them, both students and, often, faculty. (A very rough figure would be that for every forty people who apply to some institution of higher education, one graduates.) The undergraduate academic program, with its assumption that only the cognitive matters and the affective is evil or unimportant, is a source of much student protest, at least as a hidden agenda item.

Our analysis of cultural factors would suggest that it is highly unlikely that the strategy of appealing to institutional loyalty will be a good strategy for dealing with either students, who are becoming increasingly autonomous and independent, or faculty, whose loyalty is often much more with the learned societies of which they are members and which give them their rewards. There will be little personal or institutional trust in the 1970s. It is also clear that the buffers which have traditionally held off political pressures from the campus will tend to become conduits, transmitting pressure directly to the campus. In fact, the presidency of some state colleges may become not an office held by a person representing the top of the on-campus intellectual hierarchy, but one representing a branch of the state political system. (S. I. Hayakawa, who cannot command a majority of his own faculty on any issue except perhaps that of his own resignation, clearly serves at the pleasure of his off-campus constituencies only. He may represent a mutant anomaly, and he may represent a trend.)

At the same time, a word must be said concerning the diversity of campuses, in terms of both students and governance. On students, seniors at some institutions know less than entering freshmen at other institutions. While it is clear that the number of students who live according to the new value system described above is growing, the majority probably still have a clear commitment to vocationalism and to a concern for getting into college and for getting out. While there are institutions in which the drug scene arouses no interest—the decision to smoke pot or not having become a purely personal issue—there are other institutions in which the major ethical question of the day is whether girls should be permitted to wear Bermuda shorts in the dormitory social rooms.

This diversity also carries over into the way people behave in various governance configurations which require greater or less personal autonomy. For example, one study develops institutional profiles in the areas (among others) of concern for undergraduate education, commitment to democratic governance, and institutional esprit. Antioch College scores very high on commitment to democratic governance and undergraduate education and very low on institutional esprit, while a military college scores very low on democratic governance and undergraduate education and very high on institutional esprit. Antioch people would undoubtedly find the military college environment and governance repressive and intolerable, while the military personnel would be equally ill at ease in the swinging, permissive Antioch scene.

This suggests that there is no one ideal form or structure of governance which can be exported to any institution of any size and mission. The easiest answer is that the "flatter" the structure of governance (the fewer the levels between governor and governed), the more democratic the system. The data from the AAHE Campus Governance Project indicate that the situation is much more complex—if people wish to, they can be dishonest and deceitful with each other regardless of the height of the governance hierarchy. Dewey is certainly at least partially right—democratic government is a *reciprocal* way for people to deal with each other. This fact transcends structure. There is no structure which will force people to trust each other, although some structures may facilitate communication and trust, at least for certain types of people.

The 1970s will clearly be a time in which interpersonal trust will be at a low ebb in most sectors of our society. This will mean an increase in the number of adversary configurations in governance. It will also mean that faith in the idea of representation as a governance model ("I voted for Jim, so Jim speaks for me") will be in a decline. The concept of collective negotiations, already well established in community colleges (Henry Ford Community College has given the executive dean a new title: director of labor relations), will become increasingly popular in four-year colleges and universities, both for financial gain and to increase faculty power vis-à-vis the increasingly powerful state boards. In that state boards of higher education do not trust institutions any more than institutions trust their constituents, the decade will probably show a steady erosion of institutional autonomy.

Against this background, the current effort to develop a mixed campus senate (a guess would be that well over 100 institutions are experimenting with a campus senate with faculty, student, and administration representation) would seem to be a last gasp of our traditional concept of representative participation, rather than a new configuration which would allow the participation of all of those interested in a problem. The major improvement which can be expected from a mixed senate will be in communication, not in providing a new basis for institutional loyalty and cohesion through a decision-making structure which everyone can trust. Even Antioch, which has existed for years with an Administrative Council (faculty-administration-students) whose authority is legally delegated by the trustees, is having some difficulty in getting faculty to participate in the management of community affairs; they decline on the grounds that such participation is "unprofessional" and beneath them.

During the 1970s it is likely that trustees will do a lot of learning about the institutions they have in trust. Already, many have established informal contacts with faculty and student groups. The trustee membership will unquestionably become more diverse (the Hartnett ETS study has indicated just how homogeneous trustees now are), with faculty and student representation likely, as well as representation of a broader spectrum than the Republican banker-lawyer complex which now dominates boards.[5] In that members have often been chosen primarily for their ability to raise funds, it is to be hoped that the boards of private colleges will come to see this function as their major contribution. But it is more likely that public and private boards will, as Likert has shown for industrial management, tighten up in times of stress, even though it can be demonstrably shown (in industry) that this is precisely the wrong thing to do.[6]

As trustees establish more informal linkages with campus groups, the position of the president will become even more untenable. Part of his influence, if not power, has come from the fact that he has been the primary relay between the board and the campus. Many presidents have become skillful in using this linkage, saying to on-campus groups that the board will not accept certain measures when he has not asked them. But with informal contacts established, faculty and student groups can go directly to the board without going through the president, causing considerable erosion of the president's position. A subjective guess about trustees is that they too are less trusting than in the past and that they no longer feel the classic responsibility of the board to protect the manager. This change will cause a further decline in the power of the president, and will further the factionalism which is already widespread.[7]

Out of this intense struggle for power and control will come impotent institutons, as the factions will basically cancel each other out. (As Clark Kerr put it, "For every educational giant, there is an educational giant-killer.") Perhaps the most vital question of the decade will be asked in this context—if every group is simply a competing faction, from SDS to the regents, and they all disagree over who should have the power to decide what, then the real question is, *Who decides who decides?* If one follows the labor negotiations model, one is stuck with trying to find a neutral third party for binding arbitration, which would be very hard to do. Also, the classic negotiations model has men on two sides of a table, one side representing management, the other representing labor. It is unlikely that any carpenter could make a table with enough sides to seat all the factions in a typical campus dispute. Even if they could be seated, how could sixteen factions negotiate a mutually agreeable settlement? What does "leadership" mean in this context?

At the heart of the problem of government, for campus and society, is the fact that we have drastically increased the populations upon which governments must work, but we have made almost no change in the basic configurations of governance with which we try to provide the social cement which is a necessity for all social institutions. There are too many of us, on campuses and in the country, for the old system to work unchanged. Robert Sears has put the matter well:

> *When California became a state something over a hundred years ago, it had two senators. It still has just two senators.*

> *In 1790 there were 106 members of the House of Representatives. Each of them represented 30,000 people, of whom fewer than 40 per cent were adults. In 1970 we will have only 435 representatives, and each will have to be responsive to and reflect the needs of 460,000 citizens of whom more than half will be adults. . . . There are too many children in the family and too few leadership and decision-making figures to go around. . . . Each of us now has become such a miniscule part of the body politic that we now feel as if we were of no more importance than a single grain of wheat in a million-bushel storage bin. Specifically, my hypothesis is that the major source of frustration among the young—and I include the young in mind as well as the young in years—that is instigating anti-authority protests is the shocking recent increase in our inability to gain contact with, or exert control over, those persons whose positions in society require them to make decisions that affect the lives of all the citizens.*[8]

If, as America grew, we had simply increased the number of governing *units,* we would now be a nation of 200 million Americans, each living in small towns of 1,000 people. We would probably have 150 states and at least ten presidents. But we have not chosen that path, and can never choose it now, as urbanization and high population densities are obviously here to stay. In terms of governing huge populations with a structure designed for one one-hundredth of present numbers, one can equate problems of the mayor of New York City and the president of any major public university. There is some research evidence on the impact of size. Children in large families tend to have poorer self-concepts and self-evaluations by age twelve than do children of smaller families, who have easier and more frequent access to parental attention.

Although large schools are supposed to provide *more* options for individual participation, the facts on the matter can be summarized as follows: (1) Students in small schools held an average of 3.5 responsible positions per student (members of play casts, officers of organizations, participants in athletics, and so on); students in large schools averaged 0.5 responsible positions per student. Or, every other student in the large school had but one responsible activity role. (2) Students in small schools exceeded those in large schools in having satisfying experiences related to the development of competence, to being challenged, and to engaging in important activities. (3) Students in small schools received twice as many pressures to participate, or to meet the expectations of the school, as did those in large schools.[9] These findings are consistent with those obtained from the many studies of size in factories, public agencies, discussion groups, task forces, and training-encounter groups. These studies indicate a negative relationship between size and individual participation, involvement, and satisfaction. The person in the small setting experiences a greater motivation and satisfaction in belonging, as expressed by Chickering:

> *When the number of persons is low there are more opportunities to participate per person, and thus each experiences the attractions with greater force. In task-oriented settings there are functions and purposes to be carried out which impose obligations on the participants. When manpower is low each participant has to assume more responsibilities and each becomes the focus for more obligations. Under such conditions individuals perceive more clearly the importance of their own participation and the contributions of others. Thus, feelings of loyalty or responsibility are added to the initial intrinsic satisfactions which attracted the individual in the first place.*[10]

Support for the impact of organizational size comes convincingly from a study I have completed for the Carnegie Commission on the Future of Higher Education, entitled Institutions in Transition.[11] This study reports data from 1,230 institutions on all changes that have taken place in the last two decades. Of these 1,230 institutions, 355 report an increase in student protests and demonstrations in the past decade. The single most important factor in explaining the difference between those institutions which report an increase in protest and those which do not is the size of the student body. For example, of the 135 Ph.D. granting institutions in the study, those reporting increases in student protests had a mean student enrollment of 12,014, while those reporting no increase had a mean student body of only 5,360. The same holds true for other levels of highest degree awarded. If we categorize these institutions by type of control, we again find that as the size of the institution increases, the percentage of institutions reporting increased student protests and demonstrations also increases, without exception. Even more striking, if we put all 1,230 campuses into five size categories and look at the percentage reporting increases in student protests, it is even clearer that size tells: small (under 1,000 students), 14 per cent (72 of 501); medium (1,000 to 5,000), 32 percent (154 of 468); large (5,000 to 15,000), 58 per cent (75 of 128); giant (15,000 to 24,000), 75 per cent (24 of 32); super (over 25,000), 88 per cent (8 of 9).

The enormous public university structures which are to be the major pattern for tomorrow will not go away. They will continue to be vulnerable to disruption, however, as on a campus of 30,000 people, thirty leaders can find 500 people who will support almost any cause, and 500 is enough to cause a great deal of trouble, particularly if it is a different group of 500 people on a different issue every week.

Although it is after the fact, the best hope for those institutions (and all institutions) is to consider various plans for decentralization of governance functions in those areas which directly affect the quality of life of the participants. Consider as an analogy the problem of class size. If one has as an objective of a course the personal encounter of student with student and with teacher, so that they can "rub off on each other," then fifteen students is about the most that can meaningfully participate in the class. If the primary function of the class is that of communicating objective information which the student does not have to react to, then the sky is the limit and classes of 1,000 and over are economical. (Whether this kind of class should be eliminated and replaced by technological methods is a question outside the bounds of this chapter.) But given these two extremes, it is easy to see that a class of fifty is precisely the wrong size for both objectives—it is too big for interpersonal contact, and much too small for economical imparting of information. Our governance structures, for the most part, resemble the class of fifty students.

The necessary task will be that of redesigning existing institutions so that their governance can be *both small and large simultaneously.* Current writing on decentralization expresses the naive hope that the university will go away.[12] Even if the cluster college concept, which has not caught on in a large way, were to dominate, a university of thirty autonomous separate campuses is still a university—there must be linkages across the colleges, there must be reciprocity *and* autonomy between parts and whole.

From the model of class size, we can say that the ideal governance structure would be a system in which decisions affecting individuals' lives and commitments would be made in the smallest possible units, while matters of logistics and support services should be made in the largest context available, tapping into national networks. People, from registrars to full professors, will have to get used to much more ad hoc decision-making of rapidly shifting groups. More and more "Kleenex" structures will be devised, to solve a problem and then be thrown away. The older pyramid model of governance suggested that the same structure could work to solve almost all problems. There is a widespread awareness today that different problems require different structures for their solution. To solve a problem of student discontent with a structure which by its very nature suggests that students are inferior beings, subordinate to the system, is to ask for trouble. It is also going to be more difficult to maintain a rigid line between "inside" and "outside" groups—some citizens may be more concerned with (and knowledgeable about) the community college than the faculty who teach there.

Decentralization of everything is certainly no solution to the problems of governance. *Selective* decentralization might be at least a start in the right direction. For example, many campuses now practice what could be called "general education by the registrar's office," in which the curriculum of most students is determined to a large degree by centralized requirements in general education (so much of this, so much of that). This area should be decentralized immediately to the level of the individual student and his faculty advisor. Standards for student social conduct are already being decentralized to the level of the individual dormitory, as faculty promotion and tenure decisions have been decentralized to the departmental level.

This program of selective decentralization will clearly result in more shifting memberships in decision-making groups and fewer committees that will endure forever, creating enough work to justify their own existence. But this may be the right direction for some functions to move. (Columbia Junior College in California operates with no standing committees whatsoever. Problems are dealt with by ad hoc committees consisting of almost everyone willing and concerned enough to work on the solution. When a solution is found, the group disbands.)

This model could lead us toward the kind of productive modification of our governance systems that could increase the dimension of trust and loyalty, not to the huge superorganization of the total university, but to the more meaningful subunit in which the individual participates. The people of New York City seemed to be saying that the control of schools could not be handled with the city as the organizing unit, as it was simply too large to allow for meaningful participation. Many sectors of our social structure seem to be moving toward more small unit participation in decision-making, while in other sectors we see huge new organizational entities emerging that are so new we have no comprehension of them (who, Jean Gottman included, comprehends how megalopolis works?). The trick is to begin thinking in these two organizational scales, the very large and the very small, *simultaneously.* The individual is thus a precious thing with freedom and a destiny; his participation is needed in the small units in an urgent way, while at the same time huge systems of support and logistics must be developed to serve the small units. Ideally the individual has a social structure toward which he can give affection, energy, and loyalty, with goods and services provided by the macronetwork. If we are to accept this model of the future, then one very urgent need is the development of a whole new breed of administrators who can think and feel in both the humane and logistics spheres at the same time. They will be, in the best sense of the term, cultural brokers, communicating the needs of each organizational dimension to the other. There is no genetic or generic reason why men cannot make this sort of adaptation. As Clark Kerr put it: "The real problem is not the adaptability of man, which is almost infinitely greater than we once supposed, but the suitability of institutions and their policies. The contact of civilizations, the traditional and the industrial, can be managed well or managed badly. The social management of this contact, not the adjustability of individual men, is the heart of the matter."[13]

References

1 S. Wohn and J. Shaar, "The Battle of Berkeley," *New York Review of Books,* June 1969, p. 31.

2 W. James, *The Will to Believe* (New York: Dover, 1897), p. 24.

3 J. Dewey, *Democracy and Education* (New York: Free Press), p. 101.

4 *San Francisco Chronicle,* March 20, 1969, p. 35.

5 *College and University Trustees* (Educational Testing Service, 1968). Many changes are taking place in governance this year. One recent study of 1,769 institutions of higher education indicated that the governing boards of 184 now had student representatives on standing and advisory committees; thirteen reported student representatives on the board itself. Ray Muston, "Governance Changes are Catching Colleges by Surprise," *College and University Business,* July 1969. The University of Waterloo in Ontario is taking the step of establishing a single, or unicameral, supreme governing body which will combine the faculty senate, the governing board, the administrative council, and the student government into a single policy-making group, beginning October 1969.

6 R. Likert, *The Human Organization* (New York: McGraw-Hill, 1967).

7 See my report on the campus governance data, "The President and Campus Governance—A Research Profile," to be published at the end of 1970.

8 R. Sears, commencement remarks, School of Humanities and Social Science, Stanford University, June 1969 (Mimeo.).

9 R. Barker and P. Gump, *Big School, Small School* (Stanford, Calif.: Stanford University Press, 1964).

10 A. Chickering, *Education and Identity* (San Francisco: Jossey-Bass, 1969).

11 The Institutions in Transition study was published in June 1970 by the Carnegie Commission.

12 For example, C. Foote, H. Mayer, and Associates, *The Culture of the University: Governance and Education* (San Francisco: Jossey-Bass, 1969).

13 Mimeo.

10

Daniel Bell

By Whose Right?

Quo warranto is an ancient legal challenge to authority. The thesis of this chapter is that the controlling problem of the governance of universities in the 1970s will be the resolution of a crisis in legitimacy. Legitimacy defines the authority which justifies any use of power or command. Clearly, since 1968, there has been an enormous erosion of authority. The cry of the angry student has been: By what right do you say so; *quo warranto?*

To govern is to exercise authority. Rousseau wrote, in *The Social Contract:* "The strongest man is never strong enough to be always master unless he transforms his power into right and obedience into duty." No institution can live free of the daily shadow of coercion without the freely given consent of its members. A university cannot rule by power. In fact, as I shall show later in this chapter, the university has no power other than the reluctant threat of expulsion; and when it is besieged it has to resort to civil authority, an action which, at times, serves only to confirm a rupture rather than to resolve a conflict. The lack of power makes the problem of winning assent much more a question of agreement rather than a vote, for if a minority finds a situation immoral, or is not persuaded, a vote does not provide legitimacy for action. The problem is twofold: the morality of a specific action, and trust in the institution. Trust derives from a belief in the character of an institution.

The older authority of the university (and therefore a definition of its character) was, in Max Weber's sense, a traditional authority. It was rooted in the past and sanctified by its attachment to the central value system of the society. Its role was that of expressing those values; but those values were not the ideologies of any particular social body, but the maintenance of the tradition of free inquiry and the idea of civility. More recently, and this has been particularly true since after World War II, the university has sought, again in Weber's sense, a rational-legal authority, namely the assertion of a particular expertise (as the source of rational authority) and the self-conscious service to the society in the pursuit of socially defined goals (the basis of its claim to legal support). Those definitions of the university in both senses are being challenged today—at first by the students, and in a growing voice by the faculty.

To say that the university must regain its authority is simply to say that the university must live. But as what? The problem, again, is twofold: there has been an erosion of authority in the society, and to the extent that the university is part of the society, it is subject to forces beyond its control; but there has also been a specific loss of trust because of the increasing amorphousness of the institution itself, for the question constantly asserts itself: to what and to whom does one owe loyalty? The crisis of legitimacy in the university (to the extent that it is specific and not just societal) is rooted in a loss of definition of the university: its assumption of many new and contradictory functions and its evident inability (in part because, unlike the church, the other medieval institution which parallels its history, the university has had no central self-conscious authority) to define its limitations and to fashion a structure appropriate to its purposes.

The American university has become a vast "dumping ground" for tasks which the society could not perform elsewhere. The university has not resisted—in fact, it has often welcomed—the intrusions; but it has failed to adapt its structure to the new tasks. Thus, a double problem remains: to define what is appropriate to the university, and to create a system of governance relevant to its character.

To the extent that this crisis is, at least in part, due to the foundations—insofar as the foundations have by large grants of money either lured the university to accept new tasks, or facilitated that acceptance—one must face the pertinent consideration whether the foundations can ask the necessary questions of the universities. What is clear in this crisis is that while the universities have become part of an emerging system, that system itself has had no central authority or group to raise questions about its direction, its divisions of labor, and its acceptance or rejection of specific functions. The irony is that while the leading universities and the foundations have been accused of being an Establishment, they have lacked the first requisite of an Establishment: a self-conscious acceptance of their role and the ability to provide an authoritative leadership.

Any forecast about the problems of the universities inevitably derives from a set of judgments about the relevant issues, and sources of tension, in the society. Some of these are obvious, some less so. I would like to single out five factors as central to our discussion.

First, the Vietnam War has been seen as morally dubious by a large section of the society, particularly the youth in the elite universities. Beyond the question of an immediate settlement of the war or the withdrawal of American troops is a deeper question of credibility. It is essentially this: Was the decision to extend the American presence in Vietnam, and to undertake a leading role in the fighting, a mistake in judgment, an aberration of foreign policy, hubris about American power and omnipotence, or an integral extension of the society? A significant portion of American youth has asked whether the United States is an imperialist power and whether similar kinds of intervention, overt or covert, will be made. The nature of American foreign policy, the definition of national interest, the role of the United States as a world power are all problematic today; and these ambiguities affect the judgments and commitments of young people. A significant number are wary or skeptical about the nature of America's intentions as a world power; a smaller number are already actively hostile because of their vague allegiance to the idea of a third world, to anti-Yankee and anti-colonial sentiment, or to pro-Maoist or pro-Castro sentiment, and they translate these feelings into actions on campus. The question whether the Vietnam War was "integral" to the American system, whether this country is or is not imperialist, will be one of the great ideological debates in the universities—and among historians and political scientists—particularly as the New Left cohort moves up into the professoriate. This question surely will affect the debates on whether the university should be of service to the society (as when it undertakes military-related research), and what this service should be.

Second, the blacks have become the most explosive issue on American campuses in the last few years, but although the tensions will continue and even, intermittently, increase, I think that the situation will ease off within a few years. The fundamental point is that the blacks, even now, want to be included in the society, increasingly on their terms, rather than being opposed to the society, despite some heavy rhetoric. Particularly in the universities, there is every disposition on the part of the authorities to accommodate those claims. What we are now witnessing is the familiar sociological trajectory of every dispossessed group that has suddenly been enabled to move into a society from which it had been excluded: the ability to express hostility which has previously been suppressed; the reach of subjective expectations' far exceeding objective gains; and the psychological need to assert a new group identity. The last point needs some elaboration, particularly about the college blacks. It is an interesting sociological phenomenon that a second generation which has not experienced the travails and humiliations of its elders often will become more militant and assertive as it expresses its claim and right to leadership. This is an expressive phase that is often necessary for consolidating group pride and group progress (witness the sabras in Israel). The crucial point is the *objective* change in circumstances: so long as it is real, visible, and steady (often, as sociological theorems about revolution can show, it is the abrupt halt or reversal in social advance that precipitates revolution), then subjective expectations and psychological manifestations will eventually become congruent with the reality.

In all this, there is a useful analogy with the labor movement of the 1930s, which also had its sit-ins, its militant left-wing leaders, its wild rampages, and the like. But once the mechanisms of advance were institutionalized in the labor contract, a process of accommodation developed. For the society as a whole, particularly in urban affairs, there is a need to create mechanisms of political bargaining (community control of schools is one such example), in parallel with the economic bargaining created in the 1940s and 1950s. Black studies and black control of segments of the curricula, it seems to me, are not in the long run serious issues.

Third, the most fractious and frustrating dilemmas in the immediate future will be the multiplication of domestic social problems: the environment, urban policy, housing, health, education, and so on. These have come to a head for several reasons: First is the growth in numbers. Since 1945, ninety million babies have been born in the United States; the net addition to population has been about fifty-five million (or more than the total added from the founding of the nation to the Civil War). These individuals have demanded a level of services and amenities higher than that of any previous generation, owing to our rising expectation of a minimum standard of life, at a time when the costs of services have risen more rapidly (particularly in health and education) than those in any other economic sector. The second reason is the creation of a national society. Since 1940, the United States has become, for the first time, a national society. We have always been a nation, yet not, until now, a national society—one in which change in any part of the society has an immediate and obvious repercussion in every other part. Social issues are thus more visible, and their impact more coordinated. The third reason for the surfacing of these problems is the growth of "externalities." Externalities, as economists define the term, taken together are the unintended and often unplanned impact, in short the "fallout," on third party *C* (and *D, E,* and *F,* as well) of a private transaction between private parties *A* and *B*. The result is a social cost (though sometimes a social benefit, too). The most obvious example of a social cost is air pollution—the result, in part, of the larger number of private automobiles. Externalities often call for public action and lead to the expansion of public, as opposed to private, goods. As the national society becomes more interconnected, we can expect more externalities.

Yet all this change comes at a time of triple failure. First is the failure, or lack, of social knowledge. We just do not know how to cut into the system, how to decide which expenditures have a greater social-multiplier effect than others. We do not know how to organize an effective medical-care system. We do not know how to design an effective housing project. Nor do we know how to organize a meaningful educational system. The second failure is that of government. In the decade of the New Frontier and the Great Society, we had many ideas and many programs, but the housing program, the welfare program, and the like, have been failures, in part because of the lack of administrators, in part because of political pressures which have distorted the programs, in part because of the lack of social knowledge. The third failure is the unwillingness of the public to support a tax program adequate to social needs. The Vietnam War has only masked (or exacerbated) this failure. But in truth, as the present political agitation reveals, there is great confusion about the meaning of taxes, and the government has been unwilling to educate the public about the benefits of taxation. Most people view taxes as money taken from "me" by "them," as a subtraction from income, although actually taxes are money used for the purchase of necessary public services which individuals cannot buy for themselves. In one sense, these are the failures of liberalism, or of the liberal platitudes about "government planning" and "social change." Yet these failures have also contributed to young people's disbelief in the ability of the society to provide social amenities and a livable environment.

All of these changes will come to a head in this respect: A society which has become a national society must necessarily become self-conscious about its goals, and the means of reaching them. We also know that while we can clean up the environment, provide more houses, spend more for schools, and underwrite ballooning costs of medicine, we cannot do all of these at once. We have to choose. What should our priorities be? The great political debates in the immediate future, I would predict, will turn on the subject of national priorities. And the big problem, if we are not to yield simply to organized political pressures, or to the exigencies of the moment, is to try to specify why one or another set of needs must take priority. Otherwise we simply multiply the frustrations and the loss of faith in the ability of the system to function.

The fourth factor central to our discussion is that the knowledge society or the postindustrial society of the future will urgently require a highly educated population. In the postindustrial society the university becomes one of the primary institutions because of the increasing dependence of the society on the codification of theoretical knowledge. But that is a role, largely, of the elite universities. It is true that there will be, occupationally, a greater need for college-educated persons. But in the headlong expansion of higher education, the university has become a gatekeeper regulating entry into places of privilege in the society and has begun to assume a quasi-monopoly position in that respect. Like any human institution that assumes such a position, the university inevitably becomes a target for attack.

To a considerable extent, that attack has come from the students themselves. They fear, as the German poet Hans Magnus Enzenberger has put it, "the industrialization of the mind." The metaphor is not too farfetched. The industrial revolution brought with it a new discipline and a new rhythm of work, imposed on the recalcitrant bones of a rural artisan and farm-labor class. The reaction to this imposition, in the period between 1814 and 1840, was machine-breaking, wildcat strikes, an elaborate conspiratorial image of "The Thing" (William Cobbett's word for what we would today call the Establishment), and pastoral romances about the superior and idyllic virtues of times past. To some extent, the recent student outbursts are the early struggles of the postindustrial society, which has imposed an organizational harness and a discipline based on the idea of training and narrow specialization. Over the last several years, at an earlier and earlier age, an organizational harness has been dropped on young people: in the second year of high school begins the anxiety about what college one can go to; in the first year of college comes the pressure to choose a major; in the middle year of college, the anxiety about getting into graduate school; and so on. And the draft, with its pressure on male students to remain in school, foreclosed any possibility of a moratorium—a breather—between college graduation and graduate school. (The recent influx of college graduates into secondary-school teaching, because of the draft, will probably bring about productive results.)

All of this change is reflected in the agitation to depreciate the importance of college degrees, to eliminate grades, to have freedom in the curriculum, to seek interdisciplinary work, and the like. I think that much of this is logically and educationally unsound (as I argued in my book *The Reforming of General Education*), and that what is needed is a greater degree of coherence and training in disciplines already in the curriculum. But one has to recognize the latent reasons and anxieties underlying the agitation in any prescription for change. The attack on the established curriculum will gain force, particularly as the student cohort of the late 1960s moves into teaching positions. While this attack can be a source of enormously fruitful debate if conducted in positive terms, if linked, as it may be, to the larger, fractious political issues of the day, it will be one of the major problems for university administration.

Fifth, the most diffuse but in the long run the most potentially disintegrating force in the society is what we can call "the new sensibility" in American culture. Studying the relationship between social structure and culture is perhaps the most complicated of all social analyses. Changes in the economy or technology, constrained as these are by resources and costs, have determinable consequences in a society. But the changes in expressive symbols and values, in statements about the meaning of experience, and in the codes for the guidance of behavior—the dimensions of art and imagination—are unconstrained. At times, as Ortega said, they foreshadow the social reality of tomorrow (since they are played out in the mind); but at times they remain only in the realm of imagination. (Dostoevski and Gide could toy with the idea of gratuitous murder in their novels, expressing the suppressed impulses or wishes of the psyche; the actual acting out of such impulses is a more complex matter.)

The culture of the Western intelligentsia in the last hundred years has been largely anti-institutional and even antinomian. By celebrating the self and the individual, it established the polarity of the individual versus society. It exalted the idea of the genius, or the artist, who was exempt from social convention. But these impulses, as expressed by the romantics to the surrealists, have been contained by the developing discipline of form in art. What one encounters today is a double movement: an attack not only on form itself but on any effort to find meaning in art—that is, the breakdown of boundaries and the end of genres—and what Karl Mannheim once called "the democratization of genius," the idea that self-expression and self-fulfillment, without any regard for boundaries and limits, are open to everyone. In the "cult of experience" all realms of experience must be open and explored. Everything is under attack: authority, since no man is better than any other; the past, since learning tells us nothing; discipline and specialization, because they are constricting. What results is a fierce anti-intellectualism, since what counts is feeling and sentiment, not cognition. Education, then, is not the transmission of learning, but a search for "meaningful identity," to be gained by "dialogue," "encounter," and "confrontation."

Primarily, what has been added to the anti-institutionalism and antinomianism of the past is anti-intellectualism. What is celebrated is expression rather than idea, improvisation rather than text, sincerity rather than judgment. The psychedelic experience and the drug culture, the search for the "high" and for extended awareness, are the mass manifestations of this phenomenon. As the political issues recede, it is likely that the cultural radicalism (which preceded the political, and has deeper roots in the past) will be extended. The cultist aspects of these movements (the Living Theater, Susan Sontag) will fade from fashion, but it would be a mistake to assume that the deeper impulses, particularly the anti-intellectualism, will pass. For the time being, all this is restricted to a small number, yet they are the culture-bearers of an age. Just as Rimbaud, less than a hundred years ago, prefigured the beat and hippie cults, so do the Beatles make waves for the decades ahead.

Any cultural movement is multifaceted, and some interesting new areas of creativity will probably emerge from the new sensibility. But the *social* question is not the character of the next kind of high culture, but the fact that, for the first time, a sensibility of this kind has permeated a mass which by itself is not creative, yet which presumes that its experience, its search for the true self, is as relevant as all art.

For the universities, the problem will increase particularly as the large new high school generation, in whom many of these attitudes have taken a strong if inchoate hold, comes into the colleges. The problem will be particularly acute for the humanities, where these new impulses find their widest expression.

What does all this change mean for the next generations of college youth, and for the present New Left, which is coming into the society? In any immediate sense, the ability of young people to act in an organized, disruptive way will depend, in large measure, on such immediate political questions as the settlement of the Vietnam War. The SDS itself is in disarray. But if one wants to assess the possible consequences of the attitudes described above, then one can identify three kinds of possible responses, though not, perhaps, the extent and command of numbers.

One thing we can expect is a force of urban guerrillas. Some small portion of the New Left, completely hostile to the society, have psychologically taken the steps toward becoming urban guerrillas, ready to act as revolutionary forces.[1] This position is typified principally by Tom Hayden and those who acknowledge his leadership. In Uruguay and some other countries, these urban guerrillas have already organized "hit-and-run" raids in their effort to disrupt the society. These cadres will be mobilized to exacerbate problems, maintain conflicts, and incite disruptive actions.

We can also expect to hear more from the Crazies. As frenzies recede, some small groups of *enragés,* becoming more frustrated at their inability to act, will break out in nihilistic, sometimes senseless behavior. This has been the history of ebbing movements from the Anabaptists to the Anarchists. One sees now, in such movements as the Motherfuckers and the Crazies, similar types of action. In any large sense, these are not serious. In a few specific places (Berkeley, Boston, New York), they may be responsible for very serious incidents.

The third group whose numbers will be swelling is the alienated. A larger group of young people, puzzled, angry, alienated, constitute the "mass" for the radicals. While unwilling to act in a disciplined fashion, like the urban guerrillas, or in wild fashion, like the Crazies, particular issues (the Columbia gym, the People's Park) can become symbolic and inflammatory.

How extensive are these numbers? I have little way of knowing, though the *Fortune* polls give us some clues. A more important consideration, however, and a crucial one for understanding all our problems, is less the actual number than the *change of scale.* In an arena of a thousand students, the 5 per cent who are radicals adds up to only fifty activists, and they may have little impact. In an arena of ten thousand students, 5 per cent comes to 500, and these can form a powerful striking force when the situation is favorable. Our problem is that we are living in a new change of scale.

The problem of governance is tied up with the question—increasingly an ambiguous one—of what a university is, and, more broadly, what a university *system* is in the society. One can, for the purposes of analysis, identify four functions which have been and are being performed today by the university: (1) The keeping of the traditions of Western culture and the evaluation of claims to membership in this "great chain" of learning. This function is the oldest, and it is centered in the humanities. But it is in process of dissolution. In the early 1960s, a serious debate could take place about whether Nietzsche belonged in the canon of great works to be studied in a humanities course—a debate which took place at

Columbia. Today, almost anything goes. During one of the sit-ins at Duke University a student complained (on camera during a TV news program) that his modern literature course only went up to the 1950s and did not include the 1960s. (2) The search for truth through inquiry and scholarship: the effort to assert the philosophical foundations of certified knowledge, the discovery of the laws of nature, the explication of the norms and rules which govern human behavior. These inquiries still go on, though they have become, necessarily, more technical and specialized. (3) The training of a large number of people as professionals in specific fields. A hundred years ago one learned on the job. Now, with knowledge increasingly dependent on theory, one learns in a school and then takes a job. This function has been combined with mass higher education and technical training on the junior college level. (4) The application of knowledge to social use. This task included, in earlier years, aid to agriculture; more recently it has been of service to technology and to planning.

Since World War II, the third and fourth functions have expanded enormously, for many reasons: the fact that theoretical knowledge has become more intimately entwined with applied research and development, the needs of government and industry, and so on. Whatever the reason, one sees the fruits in the multiplication of research institutes, centers, and programs in universities, the expansion of research, and the service functions.

We are now back to the root question: what is a university? It is startling to realize that we have not had any adequate definition of a university. The university is likened to an extended family, a secular church, a corporation, a community, or it is simply described as a microcosm of the society. And the multiplication of its functions leads to increasing ambiguity and amorphousness about the nature of the beast—one of the central reasons for the failure to define adequate governance. If it is like a family, then one kind of standard applies; if like a political community, another set of standards; if like a corporation, a third; and so on. It is clear that elements of all these are present, and different aspects of student behavior are responses to these different facets.

But the very fact that all these metaphors and analogies

are possible only multiplies the confusion and makes more difficult the question of asserting some justification—and therefore legitimacy—for authority in the university. There are, it seems to me, two distinct justifications possible, each (as ideal types) representing markedly different roles for the university.

The first might be called the classical model. The university is that institution in the society endowed with the special function (and the extraordinary immunity) of searching for truth and evaluating the culture. In this sense, as with Plato's dialectic, it is free to question *everything*—in theory. If it is to be true to its purpose, nothing is exempt from its scrutiny. But if it is to have the immunity from reprisal which goes with this power, it must obey the ordinance of remaining at the level of theory. Whether anything is to be put into practice is a question for the society. In this model, the university stands outside the society, and contains within itself all varieties of creeds and beliefs and all kinds of persons subject to the one qualification of competence in the world of learning and scholarship. A university, thus, is the place where qualified individuals are free to explore any question, and test all areas of human experience, in theory. The second might be called the pragmatic model. Here the function of the university is primarily one of service to the society: service in training large numbers of persons, service in the application of knowledge, service of the members of the university in government and elsewhere.

The legitimacy of each type is clear: the first, knowledge for the sake of knowledge; the second, social usage. But the limitations of each view are also apparent. If one chooses the first, then one is barred, in the role as scholar and researcher, from active advocacy and partisanship. If the second, the question is "Who shall decide?" Should the universities serve the military, or the urban poor, or the radicals? Should the criterion be simply national interest, social need, the command of money, the influence of power groups, or what?

While my formulation of the types is extreme, and somewhat abstract, the division is nonetheless real, and some choices will have to be made. One answer can be to continue what we have at present—in effect, a form of laissez-faire. Those individuals who want to work in an ivory tower can do so; those who want to serve one or another group are free to do what they want. This choice is possible, perhaps, from the point of view of the professor in the university. But what of the administrator, the foundation, the alumni, the government, and the various public claimants, those who give the money or make the demands? What choice can they make? One way out of this difficulty is to realize that there need not be an either/or choice. If we are to fashion, as we must necessarily do, a university system, then we can allow the different choices to exist within a differentiated system.

The difficulty, hitherto, has been that every institution of higher learning has sought to be, with few exceptions, like every other. What we need is greater variety, serving different aims in a differentiated division of labor. There is no reason why some institutions cannot be primarily in the service of scholarship and learning, with little need to take on added responsibilities. Some institutions can be oriented primarily to research, and others to training.

But in addition to differentiation we also need divestiture. The university has become a multipurpose institution taking on all the chores that a society cannot take care of elsewhere. When the military could not find disinterested sources of advice in industry, it created the Lincoln Lab and MITRE Corporation at MIT. When the Ford Foundation wanted to extend a system of public broadcast laboratories, it asked Columbia University to accept the responsibility (which at first it did, and then declined). When the AEC needed a manager for its Argonne Lab, it turned to the University of Chicago. When the Army wanted a cover of respectability for the Institute of Defense Analysis, it sought the sponsorship of a dozen universities. But why should the universities take on all these functions? The problem, I predict, is for the universities to divest themselves of many of these tasks; and this path is as it should be.

If there is to be a national university system, then we need to initiate more sustained thought about its desirable shape. Should graduate schools and their research preoccupations be linked with large undergraduate colleges? Should one not have two kinds of graduate schools, one for detailed research training and one for broader education? What is the optimal size of a single campus?

What kind of division of labor can be created among universities as regards concentrations in different fields? Should some kinds of research be detached from universities and lodged either in government, in nonprofit institutions, or in some kind of academy structure?

These are questions about structure and function. But if one goes further and links them to the question of legitimacy, one should, perhaps, grasp the nettle and make some further, broad distinctions. Can one give all universities, private and state, small and large, elite and mass, liberal arts and junior colleges, the same cloak of immunity and privilege that is worn in the classical model? What is academic freedom in a junior college and how does this differ from the right of a corporation employee to speak his mind about politics? Does membership in a "faculty" with its privileges extend to teaching assistants and librarians? In the present "idea" of a university we have a hollow ideology which is contradicted by a complex reality.

For the sake of argument, what would a national university system look like if divided along the lines of legitimacy that I have proposed? In effect, we would have three different systems: (1) an autonomous system of elite universities and liberal arts colleges whose justification would lie in their allegiance to the classic pursuits of truth and scholarship and who would be recipients of its immunities; (2) a large-scale system of state universities and junior colleges whose functions would be primarily professional and technical training; (3) a large-scale research and service system which would be client-oriented—to the government, to industry, to the minorities—and whose function would be primarily that of applying knowledge to technological and social situations.

The system I have outlined so schematically is open, of course, to the charge of elitism. It is subject, more seriously, to the accusation that the character of knowledge and of its application makes such distinctions false and unreal. Perhaps. Each of these arguments is debatable. But the simple point is that these issues have never been debated. If one is to think seriously of a national system of higher education, serving various purposes in a meaningful division of labor, surely we must initiate this kind of debate.

This discussion has dealt largely with deep-rooted structural problems of the social and university system. Yet there are some immediate problems of governance ahead. Among the first is the containment of disruption. While it is unlikely that we shall see more student uprisings of the scope of those in the past few years—I believe the crest has been reached—obviously there will be many new and recurrent episodes. The problem to be considered is not the scope of these protests—this is hard to predict—but the altered character of the chief organizing force, the SDS, and what this portends for the universities.

The character of the SDS has changed. Early studies of student activists, such as those by Kenneth Keniston, Richard Flacks, and Brewster Smith, portrayed them as passionate, idealistic youngsters who, looking at the evident imperfections of the society, sought to redress these evils at great personal sacrifice of time and even of career. Whatever the truth of these characterizations—and they were on the whole accurate at the time—the picture is vastly different today. For one thing, the kinds of action employed—militant, boisterous, disruptive, personally aggressive—attracted to the movement many unstable personality types for whom the attack on authority was a sanction for their own obsessive rages and the acting-out of hostile impulses. The "paranoid style" has become a feature of the SDS. More importantly, the SDS organizational form has been transformed from its early open, spontaneous emphasis on participatory democracy to a closed, manipulative cadre form of organization, ready to use deceit and violence in order to gain its end.

This trajectory of change is a product, in part, of a (justified) sense of being harassed and hunted; more to the point, it is the political logic of a group which has become more determinedly revolutionist and finds that its older, anarchist mode is inadequate to its new aims. The SDS picture is complicated further by a split in the organization which has now produced two groups claiming the use of the name: one, the faction whose headquarters are in Boston, which is controlled by Progressive Labor, the Maoist wing of radicalism; the other, using the old headquarters in Chicago, a conglomerate of Castroite, new radical, and women's liberation groups. The PL faction emphasizes the need for a "working-class alliance," and tends to be antidrug and antipornographic; the established, National Office faction thinks of students as the spearhead of a revolutionary movement.

Both aspects—the split and the change in organizational character—will reduce the size and effectiveness of the SDS. Sectarian wrangling drives away many individuals, and is a diversion of energies. The kind of commitment now demanded by SDS is too extreme for most students. Yet the rivalry between the two factions, plus the desire of both to prove themselves, may in the short run provoke more disruptions as the SDS groups seek to inflame existing issues and find new ones.

How can such disruptions be contained? We must realize that the issues of disruption and of the character of the university are one. The authority of a university is not a civil authority but a moral one. It can deal with disruptions—or the threat of disruption—not by invoking civil force but by rallying an entire community to establish common rules of common procedure. Disruptive students can be contained only by a faculty and other students, not by the police.

This is not to say that police should never be used. But calling in the police is not a last resort or a first resort, but one that may be used only after an administration and faculty and students have been mobilized on the issues. The failure of the Columbia administration in April 1968 was its aloofness, not from the SDS, but from its own faculty and students. It was the SDS which initiated the violence at Columbia by insisting that the university was the microcosm of the society and challenging its authority. After some confusion, the administration, in its actions, accepted this definition and sought to impose its authority on the campus by resorting to force. But in a community one cannot regain authority simply by asserting it, or by using force to suppress dissidents. Authority, in this case, is like respect. One can only *earn* the authority—the loyalty of one's students—by going in and arguing with them, by engaging in full debate, and, when the merits of the proposed changes are recognized, taking the necessary steps quickly enough to be convincing. During April 1968, the Columbia administration never explained its case on the issues, and it had a good one (as Roger Starr has shown in his article "The Case of the Columbia Gym," *The Public Interest,* Fall 1968). The following year, when the SDS made wild allegations about the role of the university in community evictions, they were quickly answered in a White Paper, and the agitation collapsed. At Harvard, it seems to me, President Nathan Pusey drew the wrong conclusions from the Columbia example by moving to call in the police soon rather than late, whereas he should have first sought to mobilize the Harvard community around the occupied building to condemn the seizure of University Hall.

In short, the point at issue is not SDS, for SDS is not concerned any longer with redress of specific evils or with genuine reform, but the confused allegiances of the moderate students. Without the support of the moderates, the SDS actions begin to crumble, as they did at Columbia and Chicago in the spring of 1968.

On the question of containing disruption, a crucial variable is the *style of leadership.* In situations of conflict or stress, the university, like any institution, needs a rallying symbol, and this symbol is, necessarily, the president of the institution. Clark Kerr's point (in *The Uses of the University*) that the president of a school would have to be a mediator is not so. The president needs to be active and cool and aware of the ideological currents that are running so swiftly in the schools.

One of the immediate reforms that must take place in institutions lacking structure and representation is the creation of juridical and representational bodies to deal with policy issues of the university. The university today faces a special problem. The idea of a small community of scholars (with senior common rooms and junior common rooms to mark the differences in rank) on the Oxbridge model is clearly inapplicable in the United States. Given its size and varied functions, the university today mingles a political model (as regards faculty self-governance and self-selection) with a bureaucratic model (in the relation of an administration to the students, and often in the organization of research, relation to the community). The clarification of these differences—how far the university must go in being a political community, and how much bureaucratization is necessary—is one of the most pressing problems in the explication of university governance.

Clearly the university must become, more formally, a political community. The making of policy decisions must be open, subject to debate, and to some form of confirmation by the relevant constituencies in the university. There are, it seems to me, three major areas which require exploration: (1) The structure of representation. The problem will vary from school to school. In some instances there might be a simple proportional representation between faculty as a whole, administration, and students; in other, federated institutions, there would be representation by federated unit, and so on. So far as I know, there are no studies of the range of representational structures and the rationales for each. (2) The relevant constituencies. Who is to have a voice, and of what kind (with vote or without), in university deliberations? The librarians are pressing for faculty status. The teaching assistant wants to be considered as having a faculty role though usually he is also a graduate student. Do nontenured and tenured personnel have equal voice on all issues? Again, there is here a major area in need of research and clarification of principle. (3) The division of powers. What decisions, if any, are reserved for the trustees, who are often the legal custodians of the corporation? What kinds of administrative action are subject to review, and by whom? To state these questions is to indicate again how little discussion there has been of these most crucial issues of university life.

Beyond all these large-scale problems, one crucial consideration which most people accept as metaphor, yet rarely explore in practice, has to be observed: that all these problems take place within a change of scale unprecedented in the history of the university. A change of scale is not simply a linear extension of size. As Galileo defined it, in his square-cube law, a change of size is a change in form, and consequently in institution. Most of our older discussions of rights and responsibilities, allocation of powers, and devolution of responsibilities are modeled on an organizational form whose size is of a vastly smaller magnitude than our own. It is this change of scale, in all its dimensions, which still has to be explored for its consequences.

References

[1] Witness, for example, the following argument for "resistance" by an SDS leader: "The institutions our resistance has desanctified and delegitimatized, as a result of our action against their oppression of others, have lost all authority and, hence, all respect. As such, they have only raw, coercive power. Since they are without legitimacy in our eyes, they are without rights." From "Toward Institutional Resistance," by Carl Davidson, interorganizational secretary; a paper given at an SDS meeting in November 1967.

11

Ralph K. Huitt

Governance in the 1970s

The problems of university governance grow at a rapid rate, punctuated by the departures of university governors. In the late summer of 1969, it seemed possible that the wave of what is euphemistically referred to as "student unrest" might have crested and that a more peaceful year might lie ahead. A year later that happy prospect had proved to be misleading. Many institutions had closed their academic year in haste and disarray and few were not affected in some degree by the year of tumult and tragedy drawing to a nightmare close. Long-range plans for governance were put aside for examining of the immediate issue: Could the institution be kept open throughout the academic year of 1970–1971? Higher education associations held special summer meetings of the presidents of their member institutions. These meetings focused solely on that question. No one considered what to do if an institution were shut down in the middle of the year; that was a threat too grim to contemplate. The assumption of continuity had to be made. And so must it be made by the author—that the crisis would be met and the problems of university governance might reasonably be considered in a time frame of at least a decade.

Inasmuch as I am not alone in this venture, let me confine myself to the kind of institution I know best: the public university. I am concerned here not with just any institution which calls itself a university, but with one or more in each state, supported by the public, which seriously undertake graduate and professional training; whose professors are expected, at least, to make some contribution to their fields; which are first-rate or have hopes, however forlorn, of being so some day. In this kind of institution I am both an insider and an outsider: an insider from the many years spent there as graduate student and teacher; an outsider because I have not shared the crisis years as either. The distinction is important. The people who teach in and administer the universities seem, from my conversations with them, to perceive what is happening quite differently from those not on the campus—and the perceptual gap cannot be bridged by empathy alone. I am aware that in my gut reactions it is really newsprint and TV images to which I am reacting. Therefore I have more confidence in my grasp of the problems of university governance, which are long-standing, than in my sensitivity to what must be done first and what, indeed, it is possible to do.

The task I have set myself therefore is to survey the network of relationships which the administration of a public university—the president and his operating associates—must keep in some order. This is the job of the administration—not of the faculty or of any "community of scholars" which may emerge. My assumption is that in the state institutions, at least, there will always be someone who can be held to account, someone who can be fired. It is from the vantage point of these responsible expendables that I look at the clusters of relationships which must be reshaped and stabilized.

And this is a good place to begin. There has been a revolution, explosive and abrupt, in the requirements of a president and his staff. Twenty years ago professors looked with often ill-disguised condescension on administrators—even the president; they were glad lesser men were willing to take the job. Perhaps they were right; the job did not require so much then. Lord Bryce once wrote that the presidency of the United States required the talents of a middling railroad executive; and that remark, appropriately scaled down, might have fit a university presidency two decades ago. Not so today. Most bright young persons can master the intricacies of academic specialties and some can even learn to teach, but the balance of skills and courage and temperament a man needs to run a good university today are out of the reach of most. Posts at illustrious schools stand vacant, attesting to the well-founded modesty of potential candidates. When the test came some of the old breed proved to be tough and smart enough, but some did not, and the new breed has not been produced yet.

What would the first-rate public university president face? State institutions today are deeply involved with state and national governments. The federal government is (as it is with sister private institutions) their hope and despair. What the bountiful hand gives, it may—and does—withhold. With no clear goals for higher education or explication of its own role, the federal government nevertheless attaches strings and provisions, requiring commitments of institutional resources and shaping academic growth willy-nilly. No one familiar with the problem can doubt that all institutions of higher education must have a massive infusion of federal money, soon, to survive. But the question of the route it shall take, whether through students or directly to the institutions, is one of deadly import and could split apart the public and private sectors of higher education. The answer should be ready before the Congress is, and it should clarify, if that is possible, the role the federal government is expected to play.

That issue does not exhaust the problems with the national government, of course. Student militants want an end to research projects contributing to war efforts, present or future, and perhaps they will have their way. University administrations certainly must consider, at least, that this may be an item of controversy which might well be conceded. Leaving aside the threats of some congressmen to punish this kind of concession by withholding funds, what would the cost be? Does the unilateral forswearing of such research by some universities mean that all will forswear it? Or if all did that the government would too? And that professors would refuse to do it? Surely not. The government will develop its own research capacity or deal with private groups—or both. Research professors are sophisticated today; they know how to get money and establish centers and institutes. Perhaps the university base is not indispensable after all. And surely their reward for doing the nuts-and-bolts contracts would be the basic research grants too and the stipends for apprentices. For that matter, government employment itself is pretty attractive. The consequences for higher education are easy to guess. A truncated university, bereft of significant scientific enterprises, would cut a reduced swath indeed.

Problems with the states are more numerous. As campuses proliferate, state officials understandably want to bring about some order. Some sort of coordinating body seems to be the answer; all but five states now have a coordinating board with legal authority. But what should the coordinating agency do? Act as the governing board for all the public institutions in the state? Or provide a structure of coordination for the separate governing boards of the individual institutions? Or should there be a board for each major sector of postsecondary education to govern (or coordinate) respectively the universities, four-year colleges, community colleges, and technical schools? Anyone familiar with modern government knows that no word is easier to say and no act is harder to perform than *coordinate.* Moreover, the questions of who sits on such a board and how they get there will be ignored by a president at his peril. The character of the board and its composition are crucial; it can furnish the battleground on which the fortunes of all postsecondary public institutions are determined (and perhaps of the private too, if it administers federal grants and as the states begin to subsidize private education). If the members of the board represent the various interests of public and private higher education, they may produce a standoff, letting the representatives of the "public" decide. If there are all "public" members, the need for judicious and large-minded people is great. But no administration charged with the fortunes of a great university can leave the board alone. The tensions of the legislative chamber may be transferred here a hundredfold.

The board of regents is another matter. Many state legislators (and congressmen) are upset by campus disorders and believe permissive administrations are to blame. They would intervene in a minute if they only know what to do. Needless to say, many of their constituents spur them on. The regents can serve as invaluable mediators, keeping the administration alert to the pressures downtown, explaining the university to the politicians and the public. But the role of broker is not easy. Sensitivity to political heat may impel regents to intervene directly in campus discipline to supply the requisite "toughness," violating a division of labor jealously guarded by faculties. This may be well-intentioned, but not necessarily so. Regents usually are picked by the governor and reflect his attitudes. Control of the governor's mansion for a couple of years often is enough to change the control of a board. It is not even necessary for a regent to like the university or wish it well. Regents who are elected by the people understandably pay attention to the shifting winds of public opinion. The more directly politics enters into their selection, the more will political astigmatism affect their perception of the university's interests. Either way, no university administration can regard relations with its regents as fixed; a board that was "we" can easily become "they." That is why they are treated here as a problem of external relations, although that treatment may not be fair. The evidence that governing boards, public and private, are organizing and many members are working to master their jobs suggests encouragingly that generally they may become part of the administration.

The principal constituency of the university president is his faculty. This is a truism, perhaps, but important enough to risk saying the obvious. Presidents with strong faculty support indubitably can get in trouble elsewhere, but a president with a hostile faculty needs no more trouble.

This relationship too is on the anvil. Many of the accommodations by which faculty and administrations have lived were understandings only, and they were arrived at in the years when universities grew and changed slowly. Professors commonly built careers on a single campus. Leave was not easy to get, extended leave almost impossible. Faculty members came to have a strong sense of identification with their university; they participated in its affairs and many also carried the arduous burden of its committees. Their relations with students frequently were warm and close.

At least I believe this is the way it was. So it was at the University of Wisconsin when I joined its faculty in 1950. Although Wisconsin had been a major university for a half-century, personal relationships within the department were manageable: young professors were added one or two at a time and were assimilated easily, with everyone's help. Most of the graduate students were known to most of the professors. The faculty had leadership: some deans and senior professors had earned respect and took blocs of support with them automatically. Professors walked tall on the campus and most ambitions were satisfied within its borders.

Much has been made of the "academic revolution" which has overtaken the old university, and rightly so. Generous grants from foundations and the government, coupled with the demand for faculty, have put virtual independence within the grasp of the research stars. Big departments recruit continuously, not just for existing gaps in the department but for anyone who meets its standards, even to the extent of stockpiling talent for the future. Young professors so recruited understand the game; they are lured, not by money, but by research leave and support, and by light teaching loads, which provide the conditions for success. Their loyalty tends to be not to the institution but to the discipline, where the relevant reputation is made.

This tendency applies not just to the young, of course; the model is provided by their elders. In the mid 1950s a young colleague of mine turned down a lucrative job offer off the campus.

"This is the age of the professor," he said. His assessment was accurate. There is a generation gap just the same. Many young professors are skilled in revolutionary new methods and approaches which did not exist when men just a little older than they were graduate students. And many identify with students in their demand for instant change. It goes without saying that when these faculty members are involved in the ideological and emotional problems of today, they will hardly be satisfied with the slow adaptation of the institution's tradition which was the accepted route to change in the 1940s and 1950s.

What complicates the problem and adds almost unbearable tension is the mixture of the new and the old. If all professors were academic mercenaries, at home where opportunity is, it would be simple. They could be bid for, hired and fired, and left out of account in the university's governance. But many are not, and few are completely so. Any president who proposes a plan to leave the faculty out of policy-making had better announce it from the airport. Moreover, state universities are *teaching* institutions. They are required by the state to educate at least the resident young, as many with prescribed qualifications as want to come. There is a suggestion that the university include only upper division and graduate work, a seductive idea with built-in disaster; no legislature would support the huge faculty necessary for specialized research and graduate training that did not tend the undergraduate masses. And people who teach large numbers of undergraduates are involved willy-nilly in the life process of the university—curricula, rules, the clamorous needs of students.

The key to successful faculty participation in policy probably lies in a sophisticated refinement of the representative assembly already found on some campuses—the faculty senate or some similar body. The notion of a faculty sitting in plenary session, the university president in the chair, is appealing, but about as practical as having the citizens of a Greek city-state mass for debate and voting every time a municipal problem arose. The function of the faculty in university governance is largely legislative: the making of rules and broad policy for the future. The work of faculty committees frequently equals the best performed by any legislature; the decision process in full faculty usually is as bad as the worst. Unrepresentativeness, ignorance of the subject, disproportionate attention to problems—these are inadequacies of the legislature which abound in a faculty meeting. The proper substitute for it is the representative assembly, exercising real but defined and limited powers, clear as to its function, with a membership willing to spend the time and energy necessary to make it a first-rate legislature. People who sit in it should get a reduced teaching load just as part-time administrators do.

A representative assembly of the faculty can succeed if they learn what a legislature can and cannot do. A legislature can build a solid base for policy through careful committee work—which need not be restricted to its members. It can be representative in the best sense, reflecting sentiments of its constituencies without binding members to be agents. It can provide catharsis, furnishing a forum for all causes, however infeasible. It can legitimate actions taken by others—administrators, regents—with an authority vouchsafed to no other agency. It can establish a judicial process but it cannot adjudicate; the prohibition against a bill of attainder—deciding individual cases through legislative action—is universal in Anglo-American jurisprudence and deeply rooted in our common experience. It cannot deal with a crisis or manage a sequence of actions; Congress learned long ago that when disaster impends it must empower the executive and support him. There are times when a single poor strategy, carried out, is infinitely to be preferred to several good ones, variously pursued.

There is no good reason that I know why a president cannot give leadership to a faculty legislature, or why it should not be free to disagree with him without his administration's being thereby discredited. It is not natural law that a president should preside over a faculty meeting, automatically depriving himself of the most authoritative spokesman for his administration. Nor must the body be wholly faculty; it could have student representation or it could share authority with a body entirely the students' own. The possible permutations are myriad. What matters is that function and allocation of authority be clearly understood, and that good procedures be established. The stability of a democratic system usually owes a great deal to known, approved procedures. When followed with a pragmatic sense of what is possible, they stand up under many a storm.

The most volatile element in university governance in the near future obviously is the student body. It is hard to say how much "student unrest" was triggered by and is aimed at the academic revolution I have touched on briefly. John Fischer calls it a counterrevolution, a sort of student backlash at the multiversity in which they are forgotten people. Perhaps so, but liberal arts colleges which lavish attention on their students have had their troubles too. The diffuse and local nature of the action makes assessment difficult, but it is certain that in the life of a single student generation the relationship between the university and its students has changed drastically and irreversibly.

There was a time—not long ago—when a university with thirty thousand students could still pretend it acted as a parent to its students. It could and did tell girls when to come in; what liquor, if any, could be consumed by students; what boys and girls could do in cars and at parties. It could and did punish individuals and groups several times, through separate disciplinary agents, for a single offense, on top of what a court already had done. It could and did punish students for conduct at home in the summertime.

All that now sounds as quaint as grandma's rules of etiquette. Few universities now pretend that they are surrogate parents, and few parents expect it. The question now is how far the university will go, and whether it will take further steps voluntarily. Why should the university be in the housing business at all? To be sure, there are federal grants and loans for college housing and these should be exploited. But a building, once built, can be leased, on terms set by the lessor. National park facilities work on some such arrangement; and private people buy into and sell condominiums in the parks, always subject to restrictions. If universities did not run dormitories their role would be clarified for parents, who would have to relinquish the fantasy of a home away from home, and it should narrow the range of possible conflicts between the university and its students.

Beyond that, it would open the door to the next step, the

termination of university responsibility for public order outside the classroom. Why should a president be pilloried because he called the police? This should be a routine, not a fateful, act in a university, as it is in the society at large. Some universities already get police protection from the municipality on a contractual basis, just as many more of them get fire protection.

At this point in the argument many colleagues of mine object that the police respond badly; in a word, they are brutal. And indeed, sometimes they are. But they are the agents of security for the society at large, and the middle class is just now being forced to face what the poor and disadvantaged have known from the beginning. Is it an appropriate answer to shelter the middle-class young from the rigors—and sometimes outrages—of law enforcement, even as they have already been protected from the hazards of war, as the poor and disadvantaged have not? It is just possible that the most beneficial social change to come out of campus disorder might grow from this confrontation of the affluent and influential with the minions of the law. Perhaps the privileged will outgrow calling the police names and be willing, as their fathers never were, to pay the price of trying to make the police into something better. Can education, on-the-job training, better pay, and support from an improved judicial and correction system make a real change in the character of the police? Or is their job inherently one which attracts or makes brutal men? There is no certain answer, but at every crossroad in the crisis of violence the police are a crucial element. Nothing which softens that point is in the public interest.

These suggestions for lightening the load of administration are made tentatively, not so much on their intrinsic merit as for their collateral value in clearing the decks for more deadly serious enterprises. Because the university must meet the issues raised by its students, on the outcome of those issues hangs nothing less than the character of the university of the future. If federal aid to higher education is routed in the future solely through aids to students, these issues may well become unmanageable.

At the risk of gross oversimplification I am going to try to distinguish among the problems raised by three categories of dissidents and their potential in shaping the character of the university. The categories are the university reformers, the black militants, and the revolutionaries.

The first category presents infinitely less troubling problems than the others. There are changes in the university which should be made; all university people but the blind or wholly selfish have known that a long time. The liberal arts college within the university is the principal cause of concern. Its undergraduates, and the graduate students and faculty working in its departments, have voiced the most fundamental dissatisfaction. They want better teaching, more "relevant" courses, a hand in running the show. None of these requests will be easy to provide. Improvement in teaching especially presents difficulties—problems of teacher evaluation; student participation in matters of recruitment, tenure, and promotion; the threat of a two-class faculty of teachers and researchers. But these are problems a university *should* be concerned with; they are the stuff of academic life. Innovations which are proposed are variations on established practices. None represents a venture on a wholly dark and uncharted sea. What university leadership must do, it seems to me, is to identify the student leaders who want reform and will settle for a better university and help them win—against the administration, against the faculty—so the victory is theirs and their hands are strengthened, for "student power" is much more than a slogan. It represents the urge of young adults to control their lives and environment to whatever extent they can. It represents their rebellion against the ambiguities of the social status "student." And it represents the natural drives of young politicians who are learning their trade on the campus, as they should. Needless to say, the improvisations which ultimately will harden in institutions will differ from campus to campus, but come they must.

The second category, the black militants, presents vastly more troubling problems than the others do—more troubling because of the reservoir of guilt and obligation, and because of the strangeness to white educators of the black people and their needs. No white really knows what they want, and almost surely the blacks do not know themselves. Anyone who has been a white freshman on a huge campus can sympathize without daring to believe he knows what they must feel. In any event, they have caused dislocations out of all proportion to their numbers. It is hard to see how universities can handle the expanded black enrollment envisaged in legislative proposals when they have been so upset by the handfuls now on campuses. Nevertheless, fidelity to the liberal dream demands that the effort be made and that black demands, however hastily compounded and peremptorily put, be met with patience and compassion. But therein lies a peril. Institutions are tempted to let the blacks define their needs and their role, campus by campus, risking campus ghettoes at the worst or, more likely, a tarnished and diminished educational product. The latter eventuality has already been suggested approvingly by Joseph Kraft in his column in the *Washington Post* on February 13, 1970. He writes:

> *Pretty soon college will be the place where most people finish off their schooling. It will provide the basic minimum of normal education achievement. It will be what high school has been. But the high schools, as the last rung of the educational ladder, make it possible for anybody not disturbed or disoriented to get through. They do not allow people, or at least many people, to fail. And for that purpose they give credit where, strictly speaking, credit is not due—for basket-weaving type courses such as shop and home economics. The colleges in their new role are going to have to make the same kind of allowances. They are going to have to make it virtually impossible to fail. To that end, they will be instituting—indeed they have already instituted—various courses of the basket-weaving variety. At the very worst, black studies would fit under that category. At the minimum it can be seen as a crutch for Negro students—one of many crutches bound to come given the turn toward nearly universal college education.*

If that should happen—and it seems a reasonable prediction, at the least—it would be a tragedy for everyone. It would be a tragedy for the blacks who have waited so long for higher education, only to find out it does not amount to much. It would be a tragedy for all students in college, because it means more time in school for anyone who wants to get a valid degree and young people stay in school too long already. Surely that is much of the source of genuine "unrest"—young adults in their physical prime deprived too long of a meaningful place in the real world. How much worse if they, holders of a meaningless college degree as well as a worthless high school diploma, faced three or four more years in graduate or professional school to get a degree that would count.

The third category, the revolutionaries, are hostile not so much toward the university as toward the whole social system. As a French student activist put it, they are rebelling against "the specific horrors of modern society." They are not much interested in academic reform; it is just that the university is close and vulnerable.

One is tempted to counsel patience and let them destroy themselves—an operation for which they have a demonstrated capacity. But that will not do; it is their activities which tar all student protest and incite the hostility of the general public and their assembled representatives. More than that, many students who are not revolutionaries are nonetheless alienated from society and frustrated by their campus lives; in a sense the revolutionaries speak for them. They need a more expansive life, with more passion and action, and an opportunity to strike a blow at what they perceive to be hypocrisy and injustice. All this should be made available to them.

But I do not mean that it is the obligation of the university to make all this available to them. The university should have the pride and self-confidence to entertain some humility about what it can and cannot do. It is no more a substitute society than it is a surrogate family. Many young people can learn better what they need to know in a technical or business college; get more social adventure in VISTA, Teacher Corps, or Peace Corps (if they were made freely available to undergraduates); find their own identity more surely in travel or loafing. Why not provide a wide range of different opportunities? A government loan for a trip abroad, as well as for college? Or a year of personal discovery, just knocking around? (Needless to say, the idiocies of a draft system which forces qualified youth into college should be eliminated.) We are quite right to insist as a basic value of American life that every citizen has the right to the education he needs to fulfill himself. But that does not automatically translate into a college degree for everyone. Not "higher" education (which sounds like college only) but "post-secondary" education should be the aim. We are denying young people their right to be individuals and creating an increasingly explosive situation by stuffing kids into college buildings—ready and willing, or not.

Peace and order must be restored to the campuses. This is a minimum requisite of governance. University leadership already has paid a heavy price in public respect because of its inability so far to bring this about. The price is reflected in the niggling restrictions legislatures are placing on university leadership as well as in lowered appropriations. But maintaining law and order is merely a means to the central end of preserving the integrity of what is governed. I return therefore to the basic argument that university leadership should identify the roles and functions of the university, win acceptance for them on the campus and in the larger community, and stick with them no matter what.

A university can no more meet all the needs of young adults than government can create a great society. But it can provide a climate and resources for some—many, most—young people to enhance their capacity to live and produce creatively. That contribution is of a high order, so precious that we must not allow it to be destroyed or inundated.

12

Earl J. McGrath

Who Should Have the Power?

Webster defines *power* as "the ability to control others; influence, authority, or sway." There are more legalistic connotations of the term, but they are less applicable in the present context because much of the power exercised in academic institutions rests on neither statutory nor constitutional foundations. Hence, in this discussion the term *power* refers to the ability of various individuals and groups in the academic community to control the policy-making processes through specifically vested or delegated authority or through influence acquired by mere force of circumstance.

In order to determine who should have the power in the academic community, it will be instructive to look at various places where power is presently concentrated. In a strictly legal sense the most important policy-making powers in most institutions of higher education rest in the board of trustees. Charters vary in the range of their specifications, but in almost all cases the trustees collectively are the controlling corporate entity. Section 4 of the Knox College Charter gives some indication of the scope of the trustees' legal powers:

> *The trustees shall have power from time to time to prescribe and regulate the course of study to be pursued in said college and in the preparatory departments attached thereto, to fix the rate of tuition, room rent, and other college expenses, to appoint instructors, professors, and such other officers and agents as may be needed in managing the concerns of the institution, to define their powers, duties, and employments, to fix their compensation, to displace and remove either of the instructors, officers, or agents, as they may deem the interests of the college require; to fill all vacancies among the instructors, officers, and agents, to erect necessary buildings, to purchase books, chemical and philosophical apparatus, and other suitable means of instruction, to establish and regulate the proposed system of manual labor, in the way which they shall deem best adapted to promote the object of said corporation, to make rules for the general management of the affairs of the college, and for the regulation of the conduct of the students, and to establish when they shall deem it expedient, and the means can be procured, professorships of law and medicine.*[1]

No one who has even the most superficial knowledge of these institutions needs to be told that in fact boards of trustees normally exercise only a fraction of these powers. Virtually every policy decision relating directly to the educational program, to students, and to faculty activities has now generally been relinquished by, or has by custom been taken from, the trustees. Even decisions on such practical matters as physical plant development and contracts with industry and government, in which the trustees could be presumed to have particular competence, are increasingly subject to the review of others.

These statements are not made in criticism of present shifts in authority. The intent is to clear out some of the almost impenetrable intellectual underbrush which covers the field of discussion when the academic power structure is under consideration. It is important to recognize who already has the power before considering who ought to have it. In principle the trustees have much. In actuality, in the setting of policies which determine an institution's essential educational character, they either have little power, or choose not to exercise it.

If order is to be restored in the house of learning, some of the trustees' actual powers will have to be reestablished and generally accepted. The main proposition in this discussion relating to the trustees is that they must represent the needs of society for various kinds of services. In doing so they cannot delegate to others the important responsibility of introducing educational policies and practices in terms of society's needs.

The administration constitutes a second unit in the academic power structure. The term *administration* as used here refers primarily to the top educational executive—the president, chancellor, vice-chancellor, principal, or rector—and his immediate staff. This office deserves special consideration in any relocation of academic power not because it is now the dominant agency, but because it is the center into or through which the various institutional forces flow.

Under existing circumstances the office of the president is the weakest element in the complex of organizational controls. The current status of the chief executive officer is an almost complete reversal of the position of his predecessors. Typically they were the servants of neither the faculty nor the trustees. Early presidents engaged staff members and disposed of them for any reason they considered proper; they frequently selected the members of the board as well, and decided what matters to bring to the board for action; presidents often described plans for the future development of the institution in public before getting approval from any one; they made budgets, fixed salaries, and often managed investments.

All in all, they dominated the life of the institution. This image of the presidency unfortunately persists among academics and the general public.

Yet, this conception of administrative omnipotence has less reality today than the Loch Ness monster. One of the most footless canards circulated in academic institutions is the idea that the presidency is a position of great and unassailable power. The most cursory review of the critical situations in which presidents have found themselves shows that in most instances they had little or no clearly defined power to deal with these emergencies.

Consider some of the difficult situations they faced: the location of new buildings (Columbia), the admission of students of inferior academic credentials (Temple and Columbia), the introduction of new "black" courses or entire curricula (everywhere), the carrying of firearms on university property (Cornell), the imposition of higher tuition fees (Temple and Indiana), the protection of freedom of speech (Berkeley), and many others. The president has no control over any of these matters except when he acts under authority specifically delegated by the trustees or the faculty, or both. Yet in many recent situations the president has had to act without the firm support of any properly constituted body because others, notably the trustees and the faculty, defaulted in their own responsibilities.

In the past the president has been conceived to be first among equals, but at present he is last among equals. Some have compared the office to that of a high-class functionary, but today many presidents cannot even be efficient functionaries because their functions are neither explicit nor firm. It is not surprising that some of the ablest, most intelligent, imaginative, and effective presidents have chosen to leave office. Each has his own reasons for quitting but no one can doubt that the intolerable frustrations and personal abuses they have had to suffer, combined with the lack of any clear definition of the functions and powers of the office, have been decisive factors in the decision. That there are hundreds of others who have stepped out of the office before a crisis arose and still others of promise in academic life who will not accept such an appointment no informed person can doubt.

The correction of the present situation calls for a review of the powers of the president. Such an analysis will show that efficient operation requires that the two principal policy-making bodies, the faculty and the board of trustees, should first be reconstituted through legally established processes. When this is done, as many final decisions as possible within the delegated areas of responsibility should be placed in the hands of the chief administrative officer. The delegations from these policy-making bodies to the president should be explicit and definitive so that many of the present time-consuming committee meetings will be avoided. With such an enhancement of the president's status and an implementation of his acknowledged powers, the work of colleges and universities may once again be brought back from chaos to order. Faculty members will be freed from time-consuming and often wasteful meetings and enabled to return to their teaching and research. Most important of all, the office may again become attractive to energetic and imaginative members of the profession.

As history shows, reposing large powers in a leader always involves the danger of despotic abuses and usurpations. A social organization must, therefore, design a form of government for itself which will make the fullest use of an executive's ability and enterprising spirit and at the same time protect itself against caprice and tyranny. To safeguard against this possibility, the committee which makes the initial selection of a new president should represent the broadest interest groups in the institution, trustees, faculty, and students, and it should investigate the personality and character of the candidate as carefully as it does his academic accomplishments. To provide further assurance that the incumbent will not acquire illegitimate power over an extended period, the president ought to serve on a term appointment, probably five years. At the end of this time a committee similarly constituted should review the record and determine whether the term should be renewed or terminated. This plan would provide enough time for a president to demonstrate his competence and his personal fitness for the office. It also establishes an automatic process by which the board could release anyone who did not meet its demands.

The third group in the academic power complex is the faculty. American institutions vary considerably in the extent to which the faculty controls the policy-making machinery. It is not inaccurate to say, however, that the faculty is the most influential body in determining the policies which give an institution its essential character. Under its almost sole control are all matters related to educational purposes and practices such as admission standards, curricular structures, course content, examinations, and degree requirements. The faculty has also wanted, and has sometimes obtained, a voice in decisions related to the planning of the campus, the construction of buildings, and the preparation of the budget. E. J. Bloustein, president of Bennington College, in surveying developments in academic management, observes that the dissolution of trustee power has changed the direction of the North American university. Regarding the growth of faculty power, he says, "As a result of the professionalization of their occupational role, as a result of the new esteem in which they're held in the community, as a result of their own development of a faculty ethos of almost a trade union mentality, faculty have refused to fit into the image of hired employees."[2]

Few members of the academic community object to this enhanced status and influence of the faculty. Some wonder, however, whether the power of control over the academic body politic is now not becoming as lopsided in one direction as it has been hitherto in another. In any event there is one aspect of the faculty's reach for greater power which deserves careful examination by all who are concerned about the preservation of the freedoms which now more than ever before prevail in the institutions of the United States.

One factor in the shifting of power from trustees, and it may be added from administrators, is the changing connotation of the term *academic freedom*. The history of the origins of this phrase, and the penumbra of customs, practices, and rights which surround it, ought to be common knowledge among all members of the teaching profession. It is the Magna Carta of academic life. It is the profession's shield against intellectual oppression, a protection wrung with incalculable pain and effort and not infrequently professional martyrdom from uninformed, biased, and self-seeking groups within society. In its most precise and most useful sense, academic freedom establishes and protects the rights of a teacher or researcher to pursue without let or hindrance his scholarly activities within his established field of competence. With due regard to decency it enables him to express his ideas on any subject within his competence, no matter how unpalatable, outrageous, or erroneous his thoughts may seem to other members of the community of learning or of the larger society. This right he enjoys not for his own personal benefit or aggrandizement, but for the advancement of knowledge and the consequent enhancement of the lot of mankind. The American Association of University Professors and the Association of American Colleges set forth the conditions of academic freedom they endorse as follows:

> *Institutions of higher education are conducted for the common good and not to further the interest of either the individual teacher or the institution as a whole. The common good depends upon the free search for truth and its free exposition. Academic freedom is essential to these purposes and applies to both teaching and research. Freedom in research is fundamental to the advancement of truth. Academic freedom in its teaching aspect is fundamental for the protection of the rights of the teacher in teaching and of the student to freedom in learning. It carries with it duties correlative with rights. . . . The teacher is entitled to full freedom in research and in the publication of the results, subject to the adequate performance of his other academic duties. . . . The teacher is entitled to freedom in the classroom in discussing his subject, but he should be careful not to introduce into his teaching controversial matter which has no relation to his subject. . . . The college or university teacher is a citizen, a member of a learned profession, and an officer of an educational institution. When he speaks or writes as a citizen, he should be free from institutional censorship or discipline, but his special position in the community imposes special obligations.*[3]

Nothing could be of greater influence in sustaining our free institutions than the preservation of the rights guaranteed by academic freedom. Members of the professions must recognize and maintain the distinction between these rights vouchsafed under academic freedom and others which, no matter how appealing they may be, are of secondary importance.

It is not my intention in this chapter to consider all the relationships between academic freedom and the various power structures in institutions of higher education. But if its effectiveness in the foregoing limited sense is to be preserved, recent efforts to apply academic freedom to other rights or privileges ought to be abandoned. Some faculty members have been making efforts to extend the term to cover aspects of institutional life to which it had no previous applicability. Through these efforts to gain additional power, they have weakened their defense of the traditional rights, privileges, and protections enjoyed under academic freedom. Their actions have excited a growing confusion about what the term means, a confusion teachers can ill afford in the light of a growing conservative backlash.

Strong arguments are being made, for example, for faculty participation in the budget-making processes, for faculty membership on boards of trustees, for a voice in decisions on the size and consequently the character of the institution, and for a sort of supervisory responsibility over a host of managerial activities. These requests are increasingly receiving sympathetic consideration by administrators and trustees in their attempts to realign institutional powers and to bring them into relationship with the realities of contemporary life. These efforts augur well for the future well-being of colleges and universities. But these new-sought rights should not be confused with those assured under academic freedom.

The last of the four groups involved in a redistribution of academic power is the student body. In the United States students have traditionally neither claimed nor had power in the academic community. The right of the student to be free to determine the substance, the scope, and the conditions of his learning experiences has not been generally recognized. In fact, after the free elective system was established in the late 1800s, the subject of student rights dropped out of the American literature relating to academic freedom. Various so-called student governments established some years ago in colleges and universities gave students some responsibilities, but not for matters of any material significance. Now, however, students are demanding a larger control over their own education and their own lives. Whatever other aims kindle the students' desire for educational reform, the right to a voice in determining the character and conditions of their education is close to the top of any priority listing. Some of the most obnoxious and persistent student disturbances have in fact occurred not because of the authorities' outright refusal to grant a specific request, but because of their denial of the students' right to engage in dialogue on the issues.

Many institutions have already conceded the validity of these particular claims by placing students on various committees. Wherever students have been brought into the academic bodies which make basic decisions on educational policies, the results almost without exception have been constructive. Whenever they have enjoyed real rather than spurious participation, their performance has usually been thoughtful, imaginative, and conscientious. Students are gaining a measure of control over academic matters, but they are as yet markedly unrepresented in deliberative bodies which determine their educational fate. Student demands for a greater voice in determining their own education will increase in scope and vigor. Those colleges and universities which decide to involve students in the determination of institutional purposes and programs will avoid the serious disruptions which on some campuses have at times virtually stopped the educational process. More important, they will put to fruitful use the imagination, energy, and dedication of a group of young people.

This sketchy review of the present location of academic power suggests a general answer to the question about who should have the power. A new set of deliberative and governmental structures is needed in which powers will be more equitably and more democratically distributed. The dominant guiding principle in this reorganization should be the idea that education is not an agency established by a society to satisfy the intellectual interest or advance the professional ambitions of faculty members, to enhance the public image or perpetuate the preferred class status of trustees, to aggrandize the stature of administrators, or to strengthen the disruptive activities of revolutionary students. Societies create and support instruments of education with the intention that their teaching, research, and public service will preserve and improve an established way of life. This purpose has always been dominant even though in the earlier periods of American history higher education may have been inaccessible to the average citizen and remote from the concerns of his everyday life. Whatever the earlier situation, there are now ineluctable reasons for bringing the life of an institution of higher education and the life of the circumambient society into a much more intimate relationship and a neater articulation. A few examples of the changing conditions of American life will show why college and university government must be radically altered.

The swiftness of technological developments since World War II has placed a high value on special kinds of services colleges and universities can render. Many such services—such as research in nuclear physics—are esoteric to most citizens. But many more are concerned with the training of highly competent workers for an ever wider range of occupations essential to science and technology. Some of the new educational programs required to prepare and continuously upgrade an adequate work force can be designed and operated solely by academic personnel. Developments since the end of the war, however, show clearly the value of cooperative educational efforts involving educational personnel and representatives of industry and government. If the new demands society will constantly be placing on institutions of higher education are to be adequately and promptly met, there must be a constant flow of reliable information between personnel inside and outside the training agencies. The influence of the various persons involved in making and revising educational policy must be reappraised in the light of these new social developments.

The changing relationships among men and nations since World War II have created a need for a parallel expansion in the teaching and research activities of all the social science and humanistic disciplines. There is a patent need for more interdisciplinary teams of specialists drawn from these fields. These teams can help governmental and private agencies in the resolution of the social problems and conflicts which now beset us at home and abroad.

Many of these problems—poverty, ignorance, sickness, aggression, selfishness, hate, greed, racial intolerance, and a host of others—have occupied the minds of thoughtful men since before the days of Socrates. But now, largely because of an increase in mobility and communication and the rising expectations among peoples, these problems have assumed a new urgency. The equitable resolution of the conflicts rising from them can be accomplished only through the unstinting exploitation of the vast resources of knowledge and skills in the humanistic and social disciplines. The investment of a negligible percentage of the hundreds of billions of dollars spent in scientific research and development in support of comparable activities in the social and humanistic fields would pay comparable dividends. But these results can be achieved only by bringing the members of the academic community and the peoples of the ghetto, the urban community, the state, the nation, and the larger company of nations into direct working relationship.

It will doubtless seem to some that this discussion has ranged far beyond the scope required to come to grips with the question of who should have the power in the academic community. On the contrary, however, more documentation must eventually be provided to support the radical revision of the relationships among trustees, administrators, faculties, students, and the supporting society now to be proposed. Enough has been said, however, to suggest that the structures now existing in institutions of higher education for making policy, for administering it, and for keeping various groups within the institution in harmonious working relationships, however effective they may once have been, are now totally antiquated. Indeed, conventional policy making and governmental devices are so inadequate for dealing with the current conditions of academic and social life that instead of enabling the institution more fully to achieve its goals, they steadily reduce its ability to do so. Some of the resources of men and money urgently needed to resolve conflicts and improve the quality of education have been dissipated in strife among groups which should have been working with singleness of purpose toward common goals. The confusion about responsibilities, the vacillations of views, the suspicions of motives, the temporizing in action reveal the need for new governmental structures. In these reorganizations the rights and responsibilities of trustees, administrators, faculty members, and students must be clearly delineated.

To bring these several groups into more harmonious working relationships to advance institutional rather than group interests, I propose the establishment or reconstruction of two principal policy-making bodies, a board of trustees and a senate. In name, at least, both these agencies already exist in many institutions. I propose, however, that these bodies be radically reorganized and so reconstituted as to achieve substantial shifts of power within the several groups they represent. Hence, if an answer is required to the question "Who should have the power?" the answer today would have to be "All should have power: trustees, administrators, faculty members, and students." All of them commit some part of their lives to the institution in which they become involved. Under the conception of a social contract they have an inalienable right to a voice in determining the policies which govern it. The amount of power vested in each group would necessarily vary with the number and qualifications of constituent members, and the depth of their knowledge. But all would be sufficiently involved in all decisions to assure the adequate representation of their own interests, and more importantly the maximization of their own potential contribution.

Consider first the board of trustees. These boards vary in size from five or six to a hundred members; in principle they hold almost the final responsibility for protecting the institution's resources and advancing its interests. Though there are some distinctive differences in such boards, by and large, they have a common social, economic, occupational, and ideological complexion. Colleges and universities draw their trustees predominantly from the top officers of business and industry, persons who by training and experience have become accustomed to dealing with large issues, problems, and enterprises in the industrial and financial world. The remarkable success of American higher education in opening its doors to those of little means, in bringing new instructional and research services to ever more varied persons and organizations, in protecting itself against intrusive forays of vigilante and other self-serving groups, and in raising the vast resources to maintain its own health and growth must be attributed to the work, the wisdom, and the wealth of these trustees. It would be hard to find in American society a single social group whose public service has surpassed that of the trustees of our colleges and universities.

Now, however, we have reached a time in our national history when it is necessary to change the composition, the structure, and the functions of boards of trustees. These boards ought now to include a considerable proportion of laymen drawn from a more representative range of citizens. This is not the place to try to settle the difficult question of numerical representation from various social groups and interests, or even to identify the latter. Suffice it to say that a greater proportion of trustees should be drawn from minority groups, labor organizations, government, and the professions other than education and a greater proportion should be women. A greater representation of faculty members should also be included. This more heterogeneous group of citizens should come closer to representing the increasingly varied needs of a rapidly changing society than have the typical board members of the past. These new members drawn from more varied economic and social groups should vitalize the discussions and energize the actions of these boards by bringing into their meetings the firsthand experiences of those who day by day face the emerging problems of a dynamic society. They should also be effective in the reverse process of describing and interpreting the institutions' aims and programs to an ever more diversified constituency.

A second group which ought to have substantial representation on the board is the faculty. With a few notable exceptions—for example, at Cornell—faculty members have not *as such* sat on boards of control. In fact, legally, faculty members have been employees of the trustees. Whatever reason existed for excluding faculty members hitherto, the practice ought now to be abandoned. Simple justice requires that a group of persons who have so wholly cast their lot with the life of an institution should have something to say about its character and destiny.

There is, however, a more overriding and impersonal justification for faculty representation on the board. Collectively the members of the faculty constitute an unmatched source of knowledge, skill, and informed judgment. It is socially wasteful not to exploit an asset of such obvious worth. Some will argue that professors are too impractical to deal with the engrossing problems which boards of trustees now face. This view overlooks the possibility that in this time of crisis and confusion perhaps the idealist looking for new goals and new devices for reaching them may be the most practical of human beings.

Finally, serious consideration should be given to plans for including students on boards of trustees. Many arguments have been made against admitting students into board meetings even as observers, to say nothing of making them full voting members. It is said that they are too young and inexperienced, that their short residency focuses their attention on matters of ephemeral importance, and that they have no continuing interest in the institution. Moreover, it is claimed that students have recently disqualified themselves for membership in any deliberate academic body by their attempts not to improve higher education through considered reconstruction, but rather to destroy it by disruption and violence.

Regrettably some of these statements have some validity. They ought to be carefully weighed in determining how students are to be selected for membership in a board or any other academic body. It is questionable, however, whether they can be considered adequate reasons for complete exclusion. Two other considerations override these objections. First, students are the only direct witnesses of one of the most important functions of an institution of higher education, teaching. They are in fact the only group in the academic community which observes teachers in action. Trustees, administrators, and the general public do not generally enter the classroom, and a faculty member who attempts to observe a colleague's teaching feels like a Peeping Tom. Sophisticated students, on the other hand, have the opportunity and the right to appraise the relevance and the effectiveness of the teaching process.

Second, students today are determined to have a voice in the reform of educational practices and academic life. They intend to agitate for innovations which will gear education more completely to the conditions of living which they idealistically envisage for the future. I believe firmly that we are now only in the earliest, though perhaps the most dramatic, stages of a general reform of American higher education. There is already evidence that the force of violent disestablishmentarianism has been largely spent. Student activists seem to be turning their efforts to more appropriate and more fruitful academic reforms. If they dedicate themselves to these goals, they can effect changes in colleges and universities which no other group has been able to accomplish. Whether the views of students finally prevail, they ought to be heard in the highest academic councils, and for this reason a selected number should sit as regular members of the board of trustees.

Such reconstituted boards with a substantial change in group representation should have responsibility for the matters which boards generally have. They should select a president, approve other appointments, keep the institution's resources in trust and put them to the most effective use, and determine the general educational purpose of the institution and the clientele to be served. Such a reconstituted board should also be able to vitalize the institution by bringing it more intimately into contact with the society from which it gets its financial and moral support.

A comparable reconstruction is also required in the superior body which at present has almost complete control over admission standards, curricular content, and graduation requirements. In the smaller institutions, decisions on such matters are usually reached by the faculty sitting as a committee of the whole. Many universities have a senate, representative of schools or academic fields, which has jurisdiction over all academic policy extending beyond the boundaries of constituent units. In some universities the senate is a steadily active body whose meetings are well attended by its members; in others it has been a giant sleeping except when pricked by the administration.

Just as reconstitution and reorientation of the board of trustees are now needed, so a similar reconstruction and a reaccommodation in the senate are required. It should be more representative of the various groups composing the entire institutional community than it is at present. The present conditions of life in the surrounding community, especially in urban centers, ought to be reviewed in terms of the kinds of educational services they require from institutions of higher education. It is essential that these services be appraised in terms of the specific problems and emergent social changes which these institutions could help in solving.

If this kind of constant awareness of the academic institution to the needs of its constituency is to be cultivated, new types of persons will have to be admitted to membership in the top academic body. I propose that some of the lay citizens represented in the board of trustees and students be elected to the academic senate.

Such a body of trustees, administrators, faculty members, and students would bring together persons of broad interests and a diversity of knowledge and experience. As the activities and spheres of influence of academic institutions spread, and as the claims for power become more intense, as has already been the case with students, it is all the more important that there be a common forum where conflicts of views on educational issues can be resolved through appropriate deliberative processes.

There will be strenuous objection on the part of some faculty members to any arrangement which permits nonacademics to participate in the determination of educational policy. There is, of course, the prior question whether the board of trustees should in the first instance have almost completely divested itself of this responsibility. Be that as it may, issues are now being raised outside the narrow sphere of educational policy-making which ought to be resolved by a more representative body including nonacademics. One example of these changed circumstances will demonstrate the point.

Faculties generally, even in state universities where under law any student with a high school diploma has in the past been admitted, have been consistently raising the entrance requirements. This erection of constantly higher barriers to college admission has caused intensely increased competition among applicants, attended by enormous frustrations and unhappiness. Furthermore, this changed policy has also closed out thousands of young people from an institution of their choice. And there is no very substantial evidence that many of those excluded could not have succeeded and in some instances have done better than some of those admitted. Studies done at the American College Testing Program in Iowa show the grave inadequacy of the most commonly used admissions criteria and the social injustice that may result from their exclusive employment. One particular study reveals, for example, that the correlations between goals and later success in various professions like medicine, architecture, and teaching are so low as to be of no significance.

These facts raise the serious question of whether such a socially significant decision as to who shall be admitted to college, and under what criteria and circumstances, can properly be left to a single social group, the faculty. Both students and the general public have a deep interest in admissions policies. If their concern is to be reflected in the needed reassessment of existing admission standards, they ought to be represented in such a review. This example is only one of many which could be given to support the view that the superior academic policy-making body ought to be reconstituted by adding trustees and students. The case for students is even stronger, because they alone have firsthand knowledge about the content and the processes of education. What students may lack in maturity and judgment they make up for in direct knowledge and a serious interest in the educational needs of their times. They ought, therefore, to hold membership not only in the senate, but also in its subcommittees on curriculum, degree requirements, and the engagement and retention of faculty members.

That such organization and membership of the board of trustees and the senate are not unrealistic is shown by changes that have occurred in the structure of Canadian universities. These institutions seem far ahead of those in most other countries in bringing academic government into line with the conditions of modern democratic societies. McGill University, after several years of discussion, has produced a new government structure which accomplishes the goals envisaged in this presentation. At McGill the board of trustees, or board of governors, as it is called there, is composed of the chancellor, a layman who is chairman of the board, the principal, five alumni, five members of the senate, and twenty-four others of diverse background elected by the governors. These thirty-seven persons have responsibility for general policies for the management of the institution. The senate is largely an academic body in which there are seventeen ex officio administrative officers, thirty-two elected faculty members, five members of the board of governors, and eight students, a total of sixty-two. There has already been some discussion of student representation on the board but as of spring 1970 no decision had been taken on this matter.

The McGill community has expressed reasonable satisfaction with these arrangements. The sole exception is the size of the bodies, which are considered by the principal, at least, to be too large for the expeditious and efficient conduct of business. Thus far, however, no one has devised an arrangement in which fewer members would still provide for adequate representation. In any event, other institutions can profitably observe the experience of McGill in this attempt to reform its power structure.

An examination of all the relevant facts and conditions suggests that the answer to the question "Who should have the power?" must be, "All the constituent groups in the academic community." This is the democratic way and, in spite of its weaknesses and halting movement, it is superior to any other. Earlier in American higher education government was monarchical. In later years it has been oligarchical, with various power groups in the faculty dominating the political processes. I have attempted to show that "who" must refer to a great number of persons in the board of trustees, the administration, the faculty, and the student body. As presently constituted and empowered, these bodies are incapable, even under ideal circumstances of vision, goodwill, and a cooperative spirit, of conducting the affairs of the institution with dispatch, effectiveness, and a minimum of social friction. These proposals for reorganization and redirection of their aggregate efforts are designed to redistribute power and so to locate it that all interests will be suitably represented and recognized. There is no time to lose if the present movement toward disorder is to be arrested and present problems solved not by force but by the rational practices of participational democracy. A more democratic form of decision-making and management seems imminent. There are unstable days ahead while these fundamental reforms are accomplished, but the long-run result should be greater stability, less misunderstanding, and more efficient operation of the whole enterprise of American higher education to the benefit of society as a whole.

References

[1] *Charter and By-Laws of Knox College,* pp. 2–5. Galesburg, Ill.: Published by the college, 1923, as cited in E. Elliott and M. Chambers (Eds.), *Charters and Basic Laws of Selected American Universities and Colleges* (New York: The Carnegie Foundation, 1934), p. 285.

[2] Quoted by P. Nagle in "H. Rocke Robertson: Man in the Middle," *McGill News,* May 1969, p. 7.

[3] AAUP and AAC, *Statement of Principles on Academic Freedom and Tenure.*

13

Harold L. Hodgkinson

A Look Ahead

As this book goes to press, we have passed through the ordeals of Kent and Jackson State, leading into the academic year 1970–71. In the opinion of many, there will be more violence on campuses during the coming year than there has been, even though the structures of campus governance have been modified in many cases to include far more student participation in policy-making at the departmental, campus-wide, and trustee levels. This being the case, it is difficult to argue that student participation in campus governance alone will reduce campus violence. The forces which pull us apart seem much stronger than the forces which pull us together.

In these essays, we have talked a great deal about participation, representation, and structures. We have talked less of the more difficult concepts which may come to the forefront in the next few years—accountability, implementation, and process. Large segments of the American public seem to be demanding that higher education begin to justify itself in terms of specific goods and services, whereas students are often saying that certification to perform these services is what must be ended in the college and university. It is unlikely that the average citizen (if such there be) will ever come to understand what a university is all about. It seems certain that academic freedom will again become an issue on campuses, and once again the citizenry will support the politicians over the academics. Internal structures of campus governance will give ground to external, politically and economically motivated forces. Yet it is almost impossible to imagine a good university which is controlled by partisan political forces.

No campus can be governed on the basis of structure alone. Trust and respect (although they are not "in" words in current social talk) are indispensable for the successful operation of *any* governance structure. The concept of accountability is meaningless unless there is general agreement that certain persons should be entrusted with certain responsibilities, and that they are capable of carrying them out. Parenthetically, it is interesting that we have shown such concern for decision-making in this volume and so little for the processes whereby decisions are implemented, or transformed into operational realities. Although it may be possible to make decisions in an atmosphere of suspicion and mistrust, the implementation of decisions is impossible without a sense of trust and confidence in others. To speak of trust and respect today is to be branded as unsophisticated, even as unintellectual, perhaps because concepts like trust and respect transcend factor analysis.

For a while it seemed as if the threat of governance from outside the campus might become the galvanic force that could weld the on-campus constituencies into a coherent unit—the common enemy is a well-known unifying factor. But it would seem that the internal groups in higher education are not equal to the task. When all is said and done, it is the faculty who must point the way, providing a focal point for moral and intellectual leadership. Yet faculties are in disarray, unable to reach any consensus in the current crises, perhaps because they have been selected and trained to see dichotomies where no one else does. There can be no intellectual center to a campus unless the faculty provides most of it—and without an intellectual center, what is a college or university?

When only one social class went to colleges or universities it was easier to trust others, since they were just like us. But with greater heterogeneity in the student population, in faculties, and on governing boards, people from very different backgrounds are now trying to work together, and are finding it understandably difficult. To condemn higher education for its failures in governance is easy, but it should be said that a truly pluralistic conception of higher education is a new idea in this country, and cannot be accomplished without some price being paid in the form of reduced security and stability. Indeed, it seems at the moment as if the forces working for an open society are losing ground to the forces promoting a closed society, in many ways similar to the Reconstruction era. But for the first time, colleges and universities are in the middle of the fight, not on the margins.

Ironically, the fact that campuses are now being torn asunder is due in part to their success, and to their importance in American life. Perhaps they matter too much; perhaps the hopes and dreams of people for higher education are too vivid and bright. Higher education will not transform American society—it will have enough trouble just transforming Johnny, whose parents may want him to emerge from college as a cultured gentleman of the world. Just as our high divorce rate may be due to our very high expectations of marriage as an ideal romantic vision, so our bitterness over young people and campuses may be just another case of great expectations. Indeed, there is much evidence that colleges and universities, like the public schools, are actually doing a better job while handling a much larger and more diverse proportion of American youth than any educational institutions in history, yet the American people seem to regard both public schools and higher education as failures. A lowered profile of expectations for all of our social institutions may enable us to see great good in them which we cannot now see because of their lack of complete perfection. They remain perfectable, no better, no worse than we are.

Index

Index

DATE DUE

JE 17 '8[illegible]			
JY 1 '85			
JY 17 '85			
OCT 2 1 1991			
NOV 11			
DEC. 9			
SEP 1 5 1993			
OCT 1 3 1993			

HIGHSMITH 45-220